*Proofreading and Copyediting*

# Proofreading and Copyediting

## *A Practical Guide to Style for the 1970's*

by Harry H. McNaughton

*COMMUNICATION ARTS BOOKS*

HASTINGS HOUSE PUBLISHERS
New York

*Library of Congress Cataloging in Publication Data*

McNaughton, Harry H     Proofreading and copyediting.
    (Communication arts books)
    1. Proof-reading.  2. Copy-reading.  I. Title.
Z254.M23      686.2'255      73–2559
ISBN 0–8038–5797–7
ISBN 0–8038–5798–5 (pbk)

Published simultaneously in Canada by
Saunders of Toronto, Ltd., Don Mills, Ontario

Designed by Al Lichtenberg
*Printed in the United States of America*

# Contents

5

# Foreword

THIS BOOK IS as close as I can come to what it purports to be in the title—a description of and report on the practical work of proofreading and copyediting. The word "practical" is important. A fully qualified proofreader or copyeditor is a technician. He may become specialized in some kind of reading/editing but he should know his way around equally well in the language and in methods of printing.

Proofreading can embrace unlimited quantities of knowledge and so there must be omissions. I've tried to cover the subject in sufficient detail for those with limited experience but also have presumed a certain level of general education. The criteria I have used for inclusions and omissions are based on long experience with that which I have observed to be least understood by most. There are fairly sophisticated points with which the majority have no trouble and there are relatively simple ones that good editors constantly fumble.

If you have acquired experience in one kind of reading or editing I ask you to keep in mind that this is addressed to a great variety of kinds of readers. At any particular time there are in the United States more proofreaders and copyeditors than there are words in this book. In addition to their personal variations their practices and problems vary.

The labor statisticians have groupings called blue collar and white collar which can be applied roughly to proofreaders. Wearing white collars, although it isn't proper in the daytime these days, are the readers and copyeditors for publishers (book and magazine), the corporations, advertising agencies and department stores. These may be fulltime proofreaders/copyeditors with limited authority to make changes but there are many situations of differing responsibility up to the point of full editorial power.

Wearing blue collars are the typesetters' readers and the frequently maligned newspaper readers. These readers are frustratingly limited in their right to make corrections. They bear the brunt of seeing that all type specifications are carried out correctly.

So in this book it has been necessary to constantly qualify. You can't tell the proofreader who is bucking for editorial assistant to be cavalier of commas or the shop reader to chase them. Proofreaders and copyeditors make up the most criticial audience a writer can address himself to. All will be intolerant of my procrastination but even the firmest rules of formal printing have their exceptions.

This is not a style book. In printing, "style" means conformity and a style book sets forth a single way of handling the subjects treated here. There are many style books of specialized and general styles. Most publishers get out their own. There is a joint one issued by Associated Press and United Press International. The big advertising agencies issue their typographic styles and supplement them with a flow of memoranda to their typesetters. Corporations set down in great detail the handling of their corporate logos and color preferences. Westinghouse recently got out a booklet telling their executives how to use simple English.

The supreme court of general style consists of the University of Chicago's *A Manual of Style,* the United States Government Printing Office's *Style Manual,* the major dictionaries and *Hart's*

*Rules for Compositors and Readers,* published by the Oxford University Press.

Enforcing conformity to style is a basic part of a reader's or an editor's duties. Where there is a consensus of authorities I have reported it but a proofreader must find and follow the style of each individual job and prevent straying within it—not try to achieve the most recognized formal usage.

This is not a reference book but I have tried to organize it so that the information is grouped in refindable places. Some subjects overlap, of course.

I set out at the start to make a book that would be readable. There have been many opportunities to drag in examples, footnotes, illustrations, cross references and other typographic clutter the textbook writers are so fond of. That is all right for a captive audience of students but not for people who get paid to read and edit. Examples are useful and often necessary but I have worked them into the text wherever possible.

There is little here about syntax and grammar. Outside of noting inconsistencies in plurality and incomplete sentences, a proofreader—if that is his only hat—should be uncommitted on the subject. When it comes to content of the copy he should be almost totally disengaged. I have included a few instances of legal restrictions as incidental information.

Copyeditors can and must make decisions—how far any particular one can go is a moot point. Copyediting can range from wadding up a press handout and trying to bank it into the wastebasket, to writing a tactful letter to an author to suggest a change.

I've dug in the field for most of my data. There are many sources of information about printing and typography, but applying their concepts to specific circumstances—particularly a proofroom's circumstances—needs the confirmation of everyday use. In the last 15 years, when the personalities built up and the dullness wore me down, I've picked up my glasses and line gauge many times and

moved to a new shop or a new city—to San Diego, Chicago,
Cleveland, Washington, New York, Newark, San Jose and Sacramento. In each place I have worked there have been some new and
some old equipment and reading customs. Previously I had been
bound for a long while to the routine of a corporation. In the
original meaning of "journeyman" it was expected of one who
called himself one that he should journey. In a world of credit-
card requirements it isn't looked upon favorably.

At the end of this foreword the first person will be dropped.
You will be on your own to evaluate my report. Everything stated
as fact has been checked but some opinions will be my own. The
report on products is an example. Take the Typositor. It's a device
for setting words by exposing each letter by eye and it's in common use. In some shops on Ad Alley in New York there are operators who compose the highest quality display lines with it. In
another operation the printers refer to it as the "mickey mouse" and
use it as a last resort to get something that will fit.

With the technology in turmoil, there is no possibility of
setting down the last word on processes but enough of a pattern
has been reached to give an overall picture of the directions of the
industry. Much of the conversion to phototypesetting equipment
and computers has been made and is in operation. Good proofreading demands aren't changed but the methods are still changing.

In all of the technology advances there is a notable disregard
of the fact that the final product is the arrangement of words for
reading. There is more about this situation inside. I hope that by
spreading some printing knowhow among the office readers and
copyeditors, and some of the proprieties of word usage among the
printers, this book will do something toward improving things.

H. H. McN.
Sacramento, California
March 1973

# 1

# The Marks

BEGINNING THIS BOOK with an explanation of the symbols used by proofreaders, editors and markup men may be a test of forebearance for the experienced. It can also get beyond an understanding of the reasons for some of the marks and disrupt an orderly presentation of all the special circumstances calling for special marks.

But novice proofreaders often get dropped into the work cold. They may be given copy and proofs and be coached on the marks as the necessity arises to use them. It has worked in the past and may continue for many readers at the white collar level for some time to come.

The most difficult part of proofreading for the photosetting devices is working from some kind of interim interpretation of what the operator has put on the tape, before the tape is processed into finished photographic type.

In order to discuss that, the chapter on jargon must be superseded and some defining done. The manufacturers of photosetting equipment call the end-product of the machines the "printout." The printers call it the "type." Some use "hard copy."

The typescript reproducing the keys struck in punching the tape is most frequently called "printout." Copy for scanners is, in effect, a preliminary printout. It can be corrected before the tape is punched.

Sometimes these overlapping meanings get so entrenched in the language that they never get cleared up, so from here on out this book will refer to photographic reproduction of type as "type" —or, if that conflicts with metal type, as "phototype."

The in-between facsimiles of the tape will be called either "printout" or the particular system producing it. For instance, the cathode ray tube systems (CRT) are figuratively printouts. They show the equivalent of printouts on a screen and corrections can be made directly by the keyboard.

Put aside these concerns for the time being. Most of this chapter is written as though they do not exist. For the moment it will be presumed that the reader is lucky enough to be reading proofs of real type or copying machine reproductions of phototype with copy marked up by traditional methods. Disregard, also, anything you know about copy for optical recognition devices.

The standard proofreaders' marks are shown in most dictionaries. There are only slight variations and we all should do our best to keep it that way. Outside of staying awake, the reader's most difficult chore is interpreting vague instructions on proofs and copy.

For the most part, editorial corrections on original copy are the same as those on proofs—usually without the marginal notations. There are a few marks peculiar to newspaper copy that will be noted.

To a reader the most important mark made on a proof is his signature. Usually it's only initials but whatever it is it certifies that, except for the corrections made, the job is o.k. to be printed. Often there is a great deal of money involved and other considerations— like the reader's job.

In the most simple of proofreading circumstances—a proof of a newspaper story that is already in the type form of the page by the time the proof is read—there are no complications. The proof is read and returned and if there are any mistakes in the correction lines the editors will possibly find them when they proofread the printed edition or page proof and try to get them corrected in the next edition. In the case of a really terrible mistake found by the proofreader he runs to the foreman or makeup editor with it.

In more leisurely printing situations there is a long series of revisions between the first proof and the final o.k. In revisions, as a general rule, a reader is only responsible for mistakes in the correction lines and for seeing that they are inserted in the correct places. He must therefore qualify his approval by showing along with his signature the information that it was a revision and from what—author's alterations, a previous reading, another reader's o.k. or whatever.

The reader may be called upon for other marks peculiar to the place where he works. Some shops want the number of proofs and kinds of proofs marked. Some want help with the bookkeeping— notations of author's alterations by the typesetter's reader and of printer's errors by the buyer's readers. In an actual printing plant the reader may be charged with giving all printing specifications— finished size, grain direction, color breakup, etc.

In periodical work there is a system known as dummying-up. The reader goes through one set of customer's proofs and writes the galley number over each paragraph. This is so that, when the proofs are cut apart and pasted into a dummy of the pages, the man who makes up the job can tell where to find the type.

In some shops all jobs, and in all shops some jobs, are given a double reading. One reader will read the job, write the numbers 1 and 2 on the proof and initial the 1. The second reader re-reads the job and initials the 2. This of course makes bitter enemies of the readers at the best. The second reader should confine himself to outright typographical errors and avoid nit-picking corrections and space juggling. On the other hand, he can't cover the first reader's bad misses by pointing them out and allowing the first reader to mark them.

It's important to use the right medium for marking your proofs or copy. Never use a pencil that can be erased. Erasures on proofs are absolutely taboo by industry-wide agreement. Anyone telling you to use a pencil is sure to have ulterior motives. The reader's superiors in the chain-of-command may cross out corrections if they don't want them made. Whoever does so must assume responsibility.

A well-organized operation, as a publisher or agency, will assign colors to different editors or kinds of editors, as green to the style editor, etc. Even foremen sometimes adopt their own—"This is the captain speaking."

This may seem trivial. Sitting at a desk and reading an unimpressive rough proof one can lose perspective. You have to get out on a pressroom floor and see the staggering piles of expensive stock shooting out of the presses on the authority of your initials to be properly worried by the responsibility.

In book work corrections are made as shown in the dictionary samples—a mark on the spot where the mistake occurs and the correction beside the line in the nearest margin. Newspaper readers more often run a line from the mistake off to some improbable spot. That isn't all bad for it calls more attention to the fact that there is a correction. In most straight text matter the printers prefer a line above the line with the correction connecting the error to the marginal correction.

The following expansion on the examples of the marks given by dictionaries is not meant to encourage deviation from the standards but to aid in interpreting the variations proofreaders face.

The *slant*. It's also called *slash, shilling, solidus, stroke* and *diagonal*. The proper term is *virgule*. It has many uses and is also a type character so if you want it actually set—as in and/or —you should make an additional note, "Set slant."

On the printed part of the proof the slant is drawn through a letter that is to be deleted or changed, although a vertical line is better. Drawn over a capital letter it means to make the letter lower case. For words that have been set in all capitals and are to be changed to caps and lower case the slant is usually used only on the first or second letter of each word. Used on the first letter it indicates all lower case, on the second letter the word is to be capitalized. Marginal correction: "c & lc" or "u & lc." A slant through a capital in original copy should be taken to mean lower case even without the notation.

A slant or vertical line is used between letters where space is to be added—as in changing one word into two words. It can indicate word space when used as part of marginal corrections but may not be understood to do so unless topped by the space sign.

On marginal corrections, where there are more than one in the same line, the slant is used to separate the different corrections.

The *caret.* Any insertion should be located by a carefully drawn caret at the bottom of the line at the point where it is to be made. The *American Heritage Dictionary* has elaborated on this by using an inverted caret above the line for apostrophes, quotes and superiors.

For marginal corrections the caret is used to differentiate between apostrophes, quotes, commas, superiors and inferiors. The caret goes over commas, semicolons and inferiors and the inverted caret, or v, under the apostrophes, quotes, inch signs and superiors.

The *dele* (pronounced dee-lee). ( ℐ ) That's the sign meaning "delete." Properly written it is similar to the shorthand symbol for the word. It's seldom properly written. It is sometimes represented by a loop in the line leading away from the type correction. It is not misunderstood that way. Written in the margin as a short loop, however, it looks like a lower case *e* which always causes mistakes or puzzlement. Readers should take time to learn to draw the mark clearly and also to print a recognizable *e.* Even then, if there is any possibility of a misunderstanding, the entire word should be written in the margin.

The dele should not be used alone. A printer is not a dentist. He can't just pull a letter out of a solid type form and leave a hole in the form. A deleted hyphen for instance leaves two choices. If a hyphened word is to become one word there should be a close-up sign around the dele. If it's to be set as two words a slant after the dele is technically sufficient but it's a good idea to top the slant with a space sign or even write "two words" (circled).

The dele is used in making space changes as the simplest and clearest way of showing what is to be done. If you want two points less space at one point and two more somewhere else, put lines at those points and write "2 in" or "+2" at the one and " $\mathcal{J}$ 2" at the other. As in the previous paragraph, don't lose sight of the fact that you are ordering adjustment of the space in a given area—in metal type a solid metal area. Space must be added *and* deleted.

Removing a rule or an underscore in copy is best done by circling it and using the line with the loop. Attempts by editors and readers to scratch out or erase a printed rule or a typed one, indicating italics, usually ends in confusion.

The *space sign* ( # ). This is the same as the sign meaning "number" or "pounds." Here again there can be confusion with the actual type character. There is a distinctly different character for the musical sharp sign ( ♯ ).

The space sign by itself means word space. Otherwise a specific amount of space should be specified. There is more on that in the chapter on measuring.

The *close-up sign* ( ⌒ ). This is probably familiar to everyone—curved lines top and bottom. It's made in the text and again in the margin. As mentioned about its use with the delete sign it should also be added to the addition of a letter. If the letter is in the middle of a word put it entirely around the letter. If the letter is at the beginning or ending of a word extend it from the letter in the direction of the word it is to join and put a slant on the other side of the letter where the word space is to be. Otherwise there is a decision to make about which word the letter is to be added to.

There is considerable abuse of the close-up sign. Amateurs

use it vertically, like parentheses, where they want line leading removed. If it is carelessly drawn it may include closing up of additional characters that were not meant to be included.

The top part of the close-up sign ( ⌢ ) means to use a ligature instead of two letters, fi instead of fi. The marginal correction is "lig."

The letters *tr* stand for "transpose." The transposition of letters and space is the most frequent mechanical typographical error. In the text, transposed letters or words are indicated by an S-curve. The *tr* is written in the margin. If the type is so small as to threaten obscuring of the letters they can be circled. That isn't advisable in controversial transpositions like moving periods inside or outside of quotes or parentheses.

If a large chunk of copy is to be transposed, it should be circled and a line with an arrowhead extended to the point where it belongs. Sometimes it will even go over to another galley. In that case it is marked "tr to galley 4." On galley 4 indicate the spot where the chunk is to be inserted and write "insert chunk from galley 3." It can get complicated enough to code the transpositions as copy a, b, c—or 1, 2, 3.

When two linotype lines are transposed they are S-circled and marked "tr" but if more than two are juggled (a condition known as "pied") it is better to avoid trying to locate them by transposition. Figure out the correct order and number the lines in the order in which they should appear, with the notation, "put in numbered order."

The transposition of a word space is done commonly in two ways. The clearest way is a full-dress markup of the error with appropriate marginal marks. Suppose a sentence ends with a space and the period up against the first letter of the next sentence—like this: "rain .The . . ."

Put a close-up sign around the n . and a vertical line between

.T and in the margin write tr/#/ and you have exact instructions. The other way is to make the same marks in the line and tr# in the margin—which is just about as good.

The *invert sign* ( 𝔖 ) is a whirligig. Even carefully drawn it's often mistaken for a dele. It means the letter or line is upside-down. This is an error that the reader should be alert for in proof revisions containing hand-set type. Yes, alert. It sometimes takes an exceptional reader to spot an inverted I or O.

The invert is also used occasionally to mean "turn" or "straighten" especially in the case of illustrations. In that case it may be better to write the word for what you want. Illustrations of merchandise in ads are sometimes difficult to place in a true position. They are usually vignetted. Since designers find it necessary to streamline toasters and radios for high-speed airflow there may not be any vertical lines to go by and you should add one on the proof to show the correct position.

Illustrators use perspective only on the horizontal lines (as in railroad tracks coming together at the horizon). Vertical lines are drawn vertically (not as the sides of a tall building coming together at the top). So if the object has a vertical line there's no problem. If it's a table with slanting legs, for instance, you have to figure out where the vertical line should be and rule it on the proof, marking it "vertical." On human figures the pit of the neck is balanced directly above the base of the spine when seated and above the ankle supporting the weight in a standing position—barring other supports.

An *inverted T* ( ⊥ ) means to push down spacing material when it works up high enough to print on the proof. It can be used also for a single letter or for a linotype slug that has worked up. This situation causes the high letters to punch into the paper and print darker while the letters above and below appear bad or missing. A reader who is unaware of this phenomenon usually X's the good lines. Turn the proof over and a line that is punching will be embossed.

The *X-mark,* literally meaning "fix," is the most ignored sign in proofreading. The catch-all way that most people use it is partly to blame. If you have access to the type, a comparison of the actual type with a proof will help in detecting the underlying cause of bad letters that need to be reset.

When someone bangs the type, battering the face of the letters, a pattern shows. Look for a scar across several lines, also crispness in the deformity of the letters. There's no point in marking an identifiable batter with an X. Put a bracket around the lines containing the battered letters and mark, "Battered. Reset."

The frequent chips of metal that remain loose on top of the form also can be recognized after the type has been referred to a few times. They usually do not require resetting. You can X them or write "clean" in the margin.

Worn or dirty linotype mats show up in repetition as wrong fonts do and if they are circled as they recur and marked with an X the operator may at least be behooved to get rid of the mat and possibly even reset the lines. In appearance they may be bolder or lighter than the other letters or have some deforming bulge or missing serif. Buyers of typesetting should insist that such lines be reset without charge. In hand-set foundry type it's battle and compromise over which of the worst worn of the bad letters will be changed.

The shop reader can cover himself by marking anything that may be bad but must keep in mind that he, or somebody, will have to reread the line because of not knowing whether it was corrected or not. A good shop will insist on operators marking all lines they have reset and will also supply transparent proofs which can be laid over the preceding proofs to spot unexpected changes.

An "X" doesn't always mean fix. A line width of 20 picas is expressed "x20." The instruction to recast lines goes: "Cast 3x."

The use of X most likely to be misunderstood is as an abbreviation for type faces. It can mean either extra or extended. There happen to be such faces as Venus Extra Bold (VXB), Venus Extra Bold Extended (VXBX), and Venus Bold Extended (VBX).

Inserts are often coded as "X" and contrarily an X through a chunk of type means to kill it.

The old traditional *paragraph mark* (¶) isn't used much anymore except as a decoration. In job work, an open box, □, often called a "ballot box" in requests for the printed symbol, means a one-em space—the standard paragraph indention for short measures. A number inside the box or alongside it shows the number of ems wanted. Current fashion makes opening paragraphs flush and succeeding ones indented.

Newspaper copyreaders mark all new paragraphs with an L-shaped mark—whether the copy is typed indented or a new paragraph is being created. Other editors use the mark, ⌐ , inside of a paragraph to indicate a new paragraph or a new line. An inverted S curve ( ⊇ ) drawn between the end of a paragraph and a new paragraph means to combine the two paragraphs into one. The notation is "run in" or "run on."

An opening bracket, [, means move to the left and a closing one, ], means move to the right. Without further amplification they mean to move everything to the margin. There are many circumstances where a move to a particular point may be wanted, in which case the insertion of a caret or vertical line at the point to which the line is to go changes the meaning of the mark to "move to point indicated."

There is enough similarity between the ⌐ and the newspaper paragraph mark L, to misinterpret the wishes of the editor in the choice between indented and flush paragraphs. One typesetter lost a large magazine account by its foreman's insistence that the paragraph marks meant "flush left."

Parallel lines ( $=$ ) or ($\|$) mean "align." The last step in approving a proof is to make certain that all lines and chunks of copy that should align do so. This is becoming an increasing error with the use of so much pasteup. Much pasteup and stripping is done by eye alone. Proofreaders may even need drafting equipment of their own. At least a fine line should be ruled on the proof showing where the misalignment occurs.

The remaining marks are abbreviations, mostly self-explanatory.

Lower case—l.c.

Capitalize—cap. "All caps" is sometimes called for when there isn't room to underline properly. The combination c. & l.c. is often written u. & l.c. (upper and lower case).

S.C. can mean either "small caps" or "see copy."

Italic—ital.

Roman—rom.

Bold face—bold or bf. Newspapers often use hf, meaning heavy face, or ff, meaning full face.

Spell out—sp. It's usually better to cross out an abbreviation or symbol and write the complete word in the margin. Sp. is enough when there is a change of style and the correction occurs several times. Some editors will merely circle a figure that is to be set as a word.

Use figure—fig.

Wrong font—w.f. Technically w.f. means the type is from a completely different face or size of type but editors and other proofreaders may use it on italics that should be roman and so forth.

Hairline—h.l.

Printer's error—p.e. (usually circled). That's a notation from the customer to the typesetter meaning the correction it accompanies is a mistake made by the typesetter which is not to be charged for in correcting the job. A p.e. is a serious matter. A very few of them in a job add up to carelessness and incompetence. Jobs that are tightly scheduled can be delayed. There is expense in correcting and reproofing the job. The reader may be tops at finding unusual mistakes or polishing jobs but he gets known to the office by the number of times a job comes back with "p.e." on it. There is a danger of being falsely blamed. Most printing buyers are honorable about printer's errors but one major New York publishing house has a bad name in the trade for consistently claiming that manuscript errors were the fault of the typesetters.

No charge—n.c. This is, in effect, the same as the printer's error. It's more often used by the bookkeepers or in connection with bad proofing.

Out, see copy—o.s.c. Used to refer the operator to the copy for omitted copy. If it's only a few words it's better to write them in. Many people have to dig back through the copy to set the omitted matter, to insert it and to read it again. If it's too much to write in, and must be marked o.s.c., refer to the ms. page or previous galley number. Operators like to have the missing copy marked "set." Such marking of the copy may mystify succeeding readers and should be cancelled after the correction has been made.

To come (kum)—TK. Since many ads are prepared with missing copy, art or prices, the space provided must have the notation in case the missing material gets overlooked. Readers also need to watch white space for pasteup material that may have fallen off.

Let stand as printed—stet. Novices love to use this one, often incorrectly. If a correction is made on the proof and crossed out and is not to be made, the crossed-out matter is marked stet and dots are placed under the crossed-out words. The problem arises when someone strikes out a marginal correction and he or someone else then decides to go ahead and make the correction and thinks stet will suffice to explain that. In all cases make no correction in printed matter as set where stet is used.

Correct—*sic,* o.k., or CQ. The CQ or o.k. usually appears in copy following or above some unusual statement or spelling and is meant to inform printers, readers and editors. Neither is meant to be set. *Sic* on the other hand is to tell the eventual reader of the published job that the preceding is an exact quote or true. It *is* to be set except in rare cases of editorial demonstration of erudition.

Don't set—d.s. This is frequent on job copy. It isn't used on proofs but saves the reader some difficult decisions on whether or not something should have been set. Copy that is to be set should be marked by size and type face.

Flush left or flush right—fl.l. or fl.r. It is better to begin to use the keyboard keys: QL—quad left. QR—quad right. There are others but we'll get to them later.

Center—ctr, ] [ or QC.

Ragged right or ragged left—rag.r. or rag.l. This is sometimes redundant to the flush left or right order. One major agency uses a little sketch of a triangle with the side to be ragged zig-zagged.

Sometimes ragged matter may have maximum and minimum line lengths specified: [x28 max., min. 24. If the minimum cannot be accomplished without letter spacing or excessive word spacing it should be ignored by readers and the editor should reword to fit.

Letter-space—l.s. Usually accompanied by a specific number of points or units to be added between letters, or a line width to which the words are to be letter-spaced. Occasional variations are let.# and l.#.

Line for line—l. for l. or 1/l. This means lines are to be set as typed or written, not run in.

Underscoring: A single line under a word or words, with no further instruction, means "set in italics." If it is used under printed matter that is already in italics it means "set in roman." If a block of copy is marked to be set in all italics, any words that are under-scored revert to roman.

Sometimes an actual printed underscore is wanted instead of italics. That requires using the single line along with a marginal note, "score" or "underscore," and the weight of the rule (point size) to be used should be added.

An exception to the single underscore rule is newspaper copy. Most papers don't have italics in their body types anyway and all telegraph copy used to come through in all caps. Some still does and the copyreaders underscore words that are to be capitalized.

A two-line underscore means small capitals.

A three-line underscore is the standard way to indicate a capital or all capitals.

Four lines are used for italic caps.

A wavy underscore means boldface but should have the "bf" on either copy or proof.

This underscoring is not to be taken lightly. Even if there is no question that a letter is to be a capital one, underline it three times. Whoever revises or corrects your proof is going to have to judge his interpretation of your corrections on your ability to make them. If you write *Nixon* in the margin and underline the *N* three times he is going to know the next time the *0* comes up that it is a cipher—not a capital *O*—because your marks are careful and professional.

Circling can mean all sorts of things, often contradictory.

Usually it means "don't set" but you cannot depend on that. Words written in the margin usually imply direct orders to insert the words. Therefore, circle instructions that may be mistaken for actual insertions. The question mark always is subject to interpretation. If one is actually to be inserted it is best to make it clear by adding the word "set." Then, to make sure the word *set* isn't set, it is circled.

Queries are always circled. The suggested correction is written with a line between it and a question mark. A line through the question mark activates the correction. An X over the whole query kills it.

Circling is sometimes used in composing rooms as a courtesy to the man who set the job when he wasn't to blame for an error, as when the reader corrects a clearly misspelled word in copy. The operator is permitted or forced to follow copy. He resents being suspected of an error that was not his.

If a proof is crowded with corrections some of them may have to be put in balloons to avoid running them together with other corrections.

Periods and colons are circled. Some oldtimers use a circled x to indicate a period.

Hyphens and dashes are thoroughly chewed in Chapter 8. Copyreaders and proofreaders should never leave any doubt in anyone's mind about what they want set. The hyphen is written as a short equals sign ( = ). The dash is written as $\frac{1}{M}$ and somewhere along the editing, typesetting, proofreading and revising process the decision must be made and the correct mark used. Expert copyeditors also indicate at the end of manuscript lines whether one word or a hyphened word is to be used by a small delete or close-up sign if any doubt exists.

A new mark in wide use but one that the dictionaries haven't adopted yet and some printers may not understand is a single or double crosshatch on a handwritten parenthesis (→). There has always been an interpretation problem on the mark and a question about whether it is to be set. Never put parentheses around a correction unless they are to be set.

There are hundreds of characters available for printing that are not included on keyboards—typesetting or typewriter. Even accents usually must be drawn on copy. Where one occurs it should be marked boldly and clearly. If there is any question of its not being understood the name of the symbol may be given in the margin. Some compromises occur for symbols not available. Accents for capital letters are usually not stocked. The ß in German is standardly expressed as *ss* in American printing. If a symbol is to be drawn, a circled note "draw" should be entered above it in copy and space should be allowed in the typesetting with a marginal note on the proof.

In the early proofing stages there are parts of jobs that will later be printed in color, reversed or screened that must be proofread and corrected before the camera work can be done. The proofs must therefore show what camera changes are to be made.

The most common is the reverse. The type is set normally but the result is going to be a negative print of the type. What appears in the actual printing is a black area with the unprinted white paper appearing to be white type. Therefore the actual printing area of the block containing the reversed type must be shown on the proof and the whole area marked "reverse." The same holds for color and screens behind type. Include the percentage of the screen, as "20% screen."

*Copy Specifications*

Still addressing the lucky readers who are reading real proofs with straight copy markup, there are four basic instructions that must appear on copy to tell how it is to be set. They are: the name of the typeface, the point size, the leading, and the measure (width of the line).

All of these must be checked by the reader. If any one of them is wrong the entire job is wrong.

Typeface identification is taken up later. The immediate problem is to discover what face is wanted. Copy markup rarely spells it out completely. Usually some form of abbreviation is used. In a typesetting plant VB usually means Venus Bold while in newspaper markup it would mean Vogue Bold. Newspapers carry a limited range of faces of distinctly different character.

Newspaper news matter is usually coded for heads. You could spend your life working on a newspaper and never need to know the name of the face used for body matter. The heads usually come in a range of about three faces.

Monotype typefaces are coded by number and a large shop like Monsen's, Chicago, will have expert markup men specifying typefaces by number. It doesn't take long to associate the number with the face.

The second specification and the third should be combined. Eight point type with two-point leading is "8 on 10" or simply "8/10." The chapter on measuring elaborates on this.

The last specification is the measure. In itself it is simply the greatest overall width of the lines. As mentioned, it should be preceded by an x (by) to identify it. There are several ways to set a line within the overall measure and they can be shown by copy markup signs on the copy and also as part of the measure. Normal full measure lines with justification by word space is shown as [x20]. Centered lines are ]x20[. Flush left or right is [x20 or x20].

Once the basic instructions—typeface, size, leading and measure—are digested the other variations and special instructions are more or less self-explanatory.

Book specifications are drawn up separately from the manuscripts and codes are used on the manuscript, referring to the detailed specifications.

Job tickets for commercial work usually contain some of the specifications, particularly the typefaces and sizes that have been used, so that when copy has been returned and corrections come in there will be no mistakes.

Newspapers using hot metal usually specify by columns, the widths of which are known. That is included in the chapter on measuring.

*Printouts and Computer Markup*

All of the foregoing is understandable and can be interpreted by the typesetters and the proofreaders. Once the computers and typewriter keyboards and computer printouts enter the picture it is necessary to substitute symbols and numbers. It gets complicated.

In order to get the many extra symbols and commands onto the tapes it is necessary that the regular keys serve triple duty. This is accomplished by an extra shift—the *supershift.* When the keyboard is ordered into *supershift* the regular keys give orders to the phototypesetting machines to make changes in measure, face, size, leading, and to the computer to store or sort. In printouts, the typewriter heads just record the keys that were struck.

Now there's no standard system for saying what any particular command means. There are several varieties of computers all of which can have specially tailored programs, several kinds of phototypesetting machines which are continually being replaced by new models and the type faces used in a particular shop must be represented by their own numbers.

Before you get frightened out of reading any more about this diabolical plot, reassure yourself that there are only the four type specifications and the most amateur of cryptographers can solve the meaning of the ordinary commands empirically if given the phototype with the copy or the true specifications with the markup symbols.

The best general information that can be given here is a sampling of coding commands in general use.

Any command for a change in type specifications is begun by a mark on the copy that will tell the operator to hit the supershift key. One system uses an arrow pointing to the right toward the codes to begin the command and at the end of the commands an arrow pointing to the left. Another begins commands with the sign best known in printing as "less than" ($<$) and closes with a "more than" ($>$). These commands may show up on printouts the latter way or as a dollar sign.

There are complicated formats worked out for setting material with frequent changes in settings but normal commands for the information on the four basic instructions—measure, face, size and leading—don't vary much. A computer normally accepts them in that order. If one is changed it will continue to use the others. Of course a correction line from the proofdesk requires all four. A command change is begun with a *c*. It can be *cg* for the Linotron's "change grid" or *cf* for the Photon's "change face."

If we were to proceed with a sampling of marks used in markup there would be so many qualifications it would become meaningless. At this point it is better to drop back to some practical examples of a few real-life effects on proofrooms.

There's a high-quality typesetting plant in New York, good

craftsmen and top readers who can read a type specification and recognize the face, size and leading by eye and whose judgments on the slightest spacing improvements or refinements are carried out without question. The shop is moving cautiously into photosetting with the versatile Alphatype and presenting the proofroom with copies of the finished phototype to be read from normal copy markup. The only new problem is interpretation of spacing orders in terms of units.

Another typesetting shop in another city has been moving into a photo operation parallel to its hot metal for many years. Its work is mixed—from good advertising typography to grinding out pulp magazine copy. The grind material is produced from general purpose keyboards and the tape fed into a computer for storing and repunching justified tape for either of two types of photosetting units. Along with the new tape a high-speed "golf-ball" IBM printer, connected to the computer, produces visual printout on a continuous sheet of 18"-wide paper. The computer programs are hand-tailored for the particular operation. Only one man and the proprietor really understand much of what goes on. The proofreaders are completely unbriefed and stumble through the meaningless commands on the printout looking for outright typographical errors.

Newspapers have too many people involved to let things get that far out of hand. The attack one made was to use the keyboard supplied with the photo system and to use conventional markup and train operators to use the proper keys to carry out the instructions. They even let the operators do their own justification. This simplifies everything for the other departments. The proofroom gets a Xerox copy of the pasted-up ad with copy marked up in conventional style.

But the dream of dropping some copy into a machine and having it reproduced immediately as a made-up type page still persists. In the meantime a compromise can be shot for—a minimum-wage typist setting type at a maximum word speed.

A newspaper that has converted to phototypesetting with

computer justification for its display advertising only, is struggling with the markup problem as all of them are. Original copy is all retyped by the advertising department—which perpetuates, and adds additional, errors. The markup department decides on type-faces, sizes and measures necessary to fit the layouts, then converts them to computer codes and the operators just hit the keys corresponding to the markup. The type is pasted up and copied and the whole accumulation goes to the proofroom. The proof-readers read for typographical errors and makeup. For errors requiring resetting, the entire job makes the circuit again—proofroom, to markup, to operator, to floor, to proofroom.

A completely converted newspaper, with no metal typesetting, operates its advertising side much the same, with the exception that some of the proofreaders have learned enough about markup to bypass the markup department for single-line corrections. Original copy is retained by the advertising department and readers must work from the typist's version. Reading to specifications is not necessary in most cases. Reasonable conformity to the layout is usually sufficient.

News markup is done by the editorial department. For straight body matter a chart of formats is provided to editorial and proofroom. A one-column, 9/10 news story is just marked "62," telling the operator to begin the story with a command to use format 62. There are format numbers from 50 through 100 for variations in widths and type sizes and to include indents for cuts. Headline styles are limited enough that only a few are coded by typeface numbers instead of names.

News matter comes right from the dryer to the proofroom in the form of phototype. The reader pulls a duplicating-machine copy but reads from the type. Errors are marked twice, a non-reproducing blue line through a line with an error and a regular proof correction on the duplicate. The type goes directly to page makeup and the duplicate back to the operators for line corrections.

Classified ads can make or break the profitability of a newspaper. They are specially suited to the talents of a computer. Beyond the setting of the individual ads, which is relatively simple, is the problem of sorting. For a single issue the ads must be sorted into classifications—Real Estate, Apartments, Help Wanted and so forth. Within a classification they must sometimes be sorted by sequence—in the Help Wanted classification the proofreaders follow the programmers, for instance. Some ads run one day, some more, some on specific days (called skips) and some indefinitely.

While this is still a report on one newspaper's system the general approach is a package used by others. Experienced readers who have never encountered the system are already being faced with it, unbriefed. The symbols used on the printout are those produced by the Versatek printer.

It isn't necessary to use a printout. The ad can be processed through the photosetter with the computer instructions on the top. It is read and corrected on the phototype and then discarded. The computer then processes the entire day's ads in position in one-column strips. It is wasteful of expensive photo paper that way but avoids errors.

The information for each ad is contained in the order blank for the ad and is shown on the printout. Each blank order sheet is numbered. The ad-taker fills in the first blank box with the classification the ad is to run under, in the next box goes the date of the edition the ad is to first appear, in the next the date the ad is to last appear. Then comes the ad-taker's number. If it is to appear on alternating days, those days of the week in the form of numbers, are circled. The sequence within the classification is next and the computer will sort it either by number or by alphabet. In some cases, the computer sequences ads according to the first word of the actual copy.

The first thing an operator does in setting a batch of classifieds is to identify himself with a code number which is of no significance to the proofdesk. It appears on the printout as something like "do 19." The next key struck orders a classified format. That means that all of the lines thereafter will be set to the standard classified measure, face, and size unless a change to another face or size is ordered somewhere in the copy. This appears on the printout as (UF. Then the computer orders commence with the striking of the supershift key, represented on the printout by <. Everything between that and the unsupershift key (>) is a code for some kind of instruction. The different kinds of instructions are called "fields." Each time a field is complete it is followed by a comma and the computer knows which field follows. If a field is skipped, the next field must be identified by a code letter. In the example *a* represents ad-taker and *q* represents sequence.

So if a classified ad order blank is numbered 9876, the classification is 301, the beginning and ending dates are Dec. 31 and Jan. 2, the ad-taker's number 31, there are no skip dates and the sequence is "proofreader," the printout preceding the text would read:

(UF <ad09876,301,1231,0102,a31,qproofreader>

The text of a sample ad might look like this:

1   (UF   (cf3,10   PROOFREADER   (QC
2   (el2   (cf7,6 Experienced, know type faces,
3   lobster.   O.S., O.T.   (QL
4   Mr. Rampone   (WS MU 6-4242 (QF
5   (ES
0000 9876 AD STORED

The opening parenthesis followed by symbols or numbers indicates normal keyboard commands. The remainder is what will appear in type. Line 1 changes the normal face to a display face number 3 and 10-point type. (QC says to center the line and start a new one. Line 2 says to insert extra leading of two points and to revert to the normal face 7, 6-pt. size. The computer decided on when to justify the line and begin Line 3 which ends with the quad left because Line 4 is to be set by itself flush left and right. That is explained by (WS for white space in the middle and quad flush at the end. Line 5 says "end short," (ES, meaning the particular ad is completed. The computer then adds its comment that it is satisfied with the instructions and has stored the ad, ready to produce in its proper order when all of the ads are in. If the computer is displeased with any of the instructions it will report, "AD ABORTED."

There are some variations possible. If the nature of the ad called for leaders in the fourth line (LI would be shown instead of (WS and in some cases the "quad middle" (QM key is used for flush left and right. To indent lines six points on each side the copy would show (it6,6.

Some parts of the actual copy in the sample ad may need some explaining. "O.S." means "over scale" which serves the double purpose of telling that the reader must be a union member and that they pay above the union scale. "O.T." means that there will be overtime available. And Mr. Rampone doesn't need to advertise for ordinary proofreaders in his shop.

Corrections in classified ads in this system are usually marked by normal proofreaders' marks. The operator begins a correction by using (UF <ac09876>. The "ac" tells the computer that it is a correction on an ad already stored. The next step is to identify the line where the correction is to be made—<LC3> meaning line correction, line 3, and the new line is typed out. The computer will rejustify and remember the succeeding lines if copy is added. The proofreader gets his revise as a completely new ad ending with "0000 9876 REPLACED."

By this time you are probably pounding your hand on the mat to signal the referee that you've had enough and are willing to ease into the reasons for marks more gradually.

# 2

# Printing Economics

FOR OBVIOUS REASONS, proofreaders and copyeditors are usually
shielded from information relating to the charges for printing and
the methods of arriving at them but at times some knowledge of
costing can have a bearing on proofdesk decisions.

The systems of charging mentioned here are the general approach but there are many variations such as estimates, firm bids
and negotiated prices.

Basically, typesetting is charged for on the basis of time con-
sumed. A job ticket is opened for the copy received and as each
man performs his operation in producing the job he enters the time
spent on it. Time is calculated in units of one-hundredths or tenths
of an hour so that the bookkeeping department can figure the price
in a percentage of the hourly rate. That rate is something like four
times the going rate for journeymen.

There are other, special charges such as for special proofing,
extra proofs, photo prints, cuts and so forth.

Although the proofreader is usually told, somewhat scorn-
fully, that his work is "non-productive" it is included in the billing
in one form or another. The most common practice is to add it as
a percentage of the total typesetting time. Some shops require

proofreaders to enter actual time. This is theoretically the fairest system but it doesn't work. There are so many variables in proofreading that clocking a proofreader meaningfully is nearly impossible.

In the small jobs that account for much of the work in typesetting plants timing is especially deceiving. Reading through the finished proof, the time-conscious can clock the reading time at a fraction of the proofreading time—how small a fraction depending on the condition of the original copy and the clarity and number of typesetting instructions. The proofreader must study and interpret everything connected with the job, whether pertinent or not, to make sure no instruction or copy is overlooked. He must read once from copy, which may be a trick of deciphering, and again direct from the proof. Managements most concerned with speed do the most careless markup of copy, thus doubling machine, floor and proofreading time.

Speed pressure always develops to some degree. There are deadlines that have to be met and there is the enthusiasm for speed developed by the high-speed typesetting processes. Most of the vaunted, fantastic speeds are theoretically maximums, great for sales pitches but rarely put to use. It is a fact that, with a computer figuring the justification, a fast typist can produce typesetting faster than it can be proofread properly.

It's always ultimately very expensive to the management that pushes for speed—either in spoiled work or lost accounts. Speed reading has no place at the proofdesk and can only be accomplished by cutting corners—neglecting the checks on spelling, division and style; skipping through typesetting instructions, and gulping words and phrases.

There is such a thing as malingering by proofreaders and there is inefficiency in such things as a lack of facility in recognizing typefaces. But pressure for speed should never influence any reader to o.k. any job until he is satisfied that he has read it properly.

Typesetting flows to the typesetters from several sources and complications are added to the straightforward charging for time of production.

The advertising agency injects the weirdest effect. An advertising agency charges for its services by a percentage rate of the charge for running the advertisement, which it collects from the publication or broadcaster. It also collects another percentage of the money it spends on production costs, paid by the client.

In effect this results in putting a premium on expensiveness. The more the typesetting costs, the more the agency makes for having it done.

There are a few accompanying economics that affect this plum. In national advertising single insertions start at five figures and go up and up as color and multiple insertions are added. Typesetting costs become insignificant. The typography must be excellent and the mistakes nonexistent. The work must be performed in one night and the proofs delivered by opening time in the morning.

The agencies' own proofreaders are outside of the production-costs coverage and, as overhead, are rewarded accordingly while being required to perform with perfection.

Annual reports are usually handled by agencies and the big ones are also in the spare-no-expense category but there is also other corporate work flowing directly to typesetters which is another matter.

A corporation is an empire of many kingdoms, usually battling each other. The typesetter must avoid trouble with comptrollers, cost accountants, copy chiefs and packaging departments, not to mention all sorts of others who have some say in buying or paying for printing. And trouble can come from too high costs if a lot of revising is done to avoid trouble with those who designed the job or made too many mistakes in copy.

The proofreader inside a corporation has less problem with pressure for speed. He may share the agency reader's responsibility for enormous expense from errors, either in advertising or packaging.

Newspapers charge basically for space, with normal typesetting supplied. The charge is per agate line of one column but sometimes there are rates by the inch. If you want the information for
any specific case you can find it in Standard Rate and Data Service reports, a series of periodicals for that purpose.

If an advertiser chooses to have a complete advertisement
prepared outside the newspaper's plant and provided to the paper
in the form of a plate, mat, velox or reproduction proof he still
pays the space rate. Most banks and some department stores do
this as do the national advertisers.

This situation brought on the controversial union requirements that advertisements originating outside of a newspaper's
plant be duplicated—reset, proofread, corrected and dumped.

Mostly the system (called "bogus") has been negotiated
away, but for all its waste it made economic sense. A newspaper
has heavy seasonal employment fluctuation and by having to re-
produce ads, with the typesetting paid for by advertisers, can level
off a more stable work force.

The present monopoly condition of the newspaper industry
will act to prevent what would happen in a competitive situation
where the publisher could not plead having to duplicate ads—a
demand by the advertisers for lower rates for prepared ads.

Magazines usually charge for space alone. Again the details
are in SRDS. The advertisers furnish art or plates. The publication
can arrange for preparation of the ads at the advertiser's expense.

Book publishers use either the complete book manufacturing
plants or have the typesetting part done in private shops. They can
usually negotiate for much lower rates than are charged for general work if work is slow in a particular shop.

When a typesetting job is submitted to a customer it is sup-
posedly free of typographical errors. Any errors found by the customer can be marked "p.e." (printer's error) and the typesetter is
required to make correction free of charge. On jobs that are delivered as reproduction proofs a single error can cause the typesetter to correct it and furnish new proofs free—sometimes

having to do it over entirely. This can make him very unhappy with his reader.

On the other hand, the customer's corrections, called "alts" or "AA's" (author's alterations), are chargeable at premium rates. Alterations are often the most profitable part of the typesetting business. It sometimes seems that original copy has had no copyediting at all.

Printers' errors, being corrected at the same time as the AA's, are difficult to separate and usually get included in the billing. This is a minor matter on jobs that are well proofread originally but there are typesetters who make a practice of taking advantage of the situation and sending out carelessly read proofs in order to charge the customers for their own mistakes. An able, conscientious proofreader may get himself promptly fired in such shops.

Usually bills for alterations are accompanied by proofs showing where alterations were made. This part of the bookkeeping is often the responsibility of the proofreader. As he reads the revised proof he indicates lines or, for hand type, words that have been reset. He also marks additions or deletions of space and type movements. A red pen, preferably felt tipped, or red grease pencil is used. Red signifies to the printers that what may appear to be a correction is to be ignored.

Overtime is an insidious economic factor that plagues the industry as it does all others. It may lead to the downfall of the ITU and has already done irreparable harm through divisiveness among the members.

Overtime is deceptive to the individual receiving it and few can resist its lure. The tax arithmetic doesn't show on those figures on the pay check and the immediate job seems very secure. Let those who could not obtain work because of it go away.

Employers have long been aware that overtime rates amount to less than sick leave, vacations, medical plans and so forth. Two employees working one and one-half shifts cost less than three employees working normal shifts. Overtime also allows for fluctuating work needs and creates a backlog of unemployed to draw on and to threaten the jobs of the employed.

The International Typographical Union has until recently had a law that its members must post their overtime and when it amounts to a full shift or more must hire the first available substitute seeking work. This law made it possible for many decades for any unemployed member to go to any shop and find immediate work until normal attrition moved him into a regular situation. It also aided in taking up slack periods. Printers have rarely needed to beg from the bureaucrats at the unemployment offices any fraction of taxes they paid.

During the years of full employment, however, overtime became a way of life with many printers and the extra money taken for granted. Now the overtime law has fallen to a token only in many cities and others have refused to accept travelers' cards. Thus a backlog of unemployed has been built which is resulting in hopelessly lost strikes.

# 3

# The Copyholder

ONE OF THE lowliest jobs in the printing industry is that of the copyholder but copyholding is the best practical training a proofreader can get and good copyholders soon graduate to become readers.

Many establishments have their readers use copyholders full time. Most do not but every reader occasionally seeks the assistance of someone to hold copy for jobs that are easier or better read with help. The copyholder may be a fellow journeyman, apprentice, proofboy, office worker or whoever else is available. Some ITU locals have a captive subordinate union for proofpress operators and copyholders.

There is some disagreement as to who reads to whom. Usually the reading is shared if there is much of it. The copyholder is responsible for any deviation from copy and therefore can be held accountable for a mistake caused by the reader's inattention when the holder does the reading. The reader is likely to be more interested in doing a good job and may want to check on the holder's dependability by hearing him read the copy aloud.

Pronunciation, or articulate utterance, is vital—and not just the kind of pronunciation presently advocated by dictionaries.

Wherever a syllable can be pronounced in such a way as to make the spelling apparent one should do so. Try it with *Mary, merry and marry:* "may-ree," "mehr-ree," and "m-a-a-r-r-ree." The last one is hard to render in print but resembles the drawn-out sheep's bleat.

The *u* is hard to show. It can be spoken the German way, as in "boorg" for *burg* as contrasted with "behrg" for *berg*. It is more difficult in *bury* and *berry* which the dictionaries would have you believe should be pronounced exactly the same. Pronouncing each *r* in "behr-ree" helps.

Some spellings are impossible to show by pronunciation and should be explained by the one reading aloud. *Sulfur* is "sul-fur-eff" and *sulphur*, "sul-fur-pee-aitch" at least on its first appearance. Both reader and holder thereafter watch for a switch in spelling.

Holding copy quickly trains one to be observant of the spelling of names, a useful habit for a proofreader. There are so many variations in names that the reader is helpless if given ordinary pronunciation.

For some names there are generally accepted code words. *Mc* is pronounced "mick" and *Mac* is "mack."

*Stuart* is pronounced "stew-art" but *Stewart* is always "stee-wart."

*Lewis* is "lou-iss" but *Louis* is "lou-ee."

To differentiate between *K* and *C* in proper names the custom is to use the *K* sound where it's spelled that way and to pronounce *C* as *S*. *Karl* is pronounced normally but *Carl* is "sarl."

*Catherine* has six common spellings and others. It can be the way spelled above or *Cathryn* or *Cathrine* or any of them beginning with a *K*. Thus *Catherine* would be rendered in copyholderese as "sath-ē-rīne."

Accents have been introduced at this point to acquaint anyone unfamiliar with them with the most useful one. It is described as "long" and means that the letter is pronounced as it would be in reciting the alphabet: *āle, ēve, ōld, cūbe, īce.*

The hardest thing to impress upon a copyholder is the fact that there are many ways to put a thing down in print and that he must read exactly what he sees—not what he associates with it. We ordinarily, without realizing it, translate as we read, filling in abbreviations, counting nine, ten and eleven for ix, x and xi, and flipping the dollar sign over behind the figure and making a word of it.

There are code words to be substituted for most symbols and signs. Some are standard but readers sometimes improvise their own. The following are recommended.

A period is a "point." A comma is the first syllable of the word, "kahm." Competent readers don't always bother with every comma and period if they are correctly used, except in legal matter.

For a question mark, the hillbilly "huh?" is good. An exclamation point is universally "bang."

Quotation marks need be nothing more than "quote" or "quotes." "Close" is better than "unquote." An apostrophe is "pause." The similar mark (') used for inches and dittoes is "dit."

Hyphens are called "hy" but where three words are combined some use the expression "three hooked-up," an unnecessary complication. Some also call parentheses "fingernails" but "pren" does the job just as well. Since punctuation used in conjunction with parentheses is usually used incorrectly it should be included even if periods are being omitted, "point, pren" or "pren, point."

One system for showing words inside of quotes or parentheses or set in italics or boldface is to count the number of words enclosed and then say (for instance as here), "four in." This can become awkward if more words are included than can be counted at a glance so it is customary to announce the beginning of a group of words set in italics and say "end italic" when the copy reverts to roman.

The virgule, diagonal, shilling, solidus or slash (/) is usually called "slant."

An ellipsis may be three or four periods. Due to its frequent misuse, explained later, it should be read as it appears, "three dots" or "four dots."

The names and nicknames of the major accents used on foreign words are as follows: (è), grave, "grahv." (é), acute, "cute." ( ∧ ), circumflex, "doghouse." ( ∿ ) tilde, "snake." (ö), diaresis, "umlaut." (ç) cedilla, "say-dee-yah."

Besides plus, minus, times and equals signs there are several other mathematical signs regularly used which can be best illustrated by an example:

$$\sqrt{a + b} < (a - b)^3 > a \times b^2 \leqq ab$$

This is read, "Root a plus b less than pren a minus b pren soup three more than a times b soup two less equal a b." The less-than sign ($<$) can be called just "less" and the greater-than sign ($>$) just "more." The last sign ($\leqq$) is actually "less than or equal to" but "less equal" identifies it.

"Soup" means that the figures or formula following are superior ones. "Sub" or "down" can be used preceding inferior characters.

The need to read Greek letters comes up often. The names of the letters are listed in dictionaries under *alphabet*.

In calling out capitalization it is best to say "caps" only for words completely in caps and use "up" for words with the first letter capitalized. Counting can be of use here: "Vice President Spiro Agnew—four up."

Tapping on the desk with a pencil while reading a word that is capitalized is a good trick. Or, if there isn't much need to explain the capitalization and something else comes up frequently, a tap can be agreed to mean that. In this chapter it might be used for italics or for quotes.

A degree mark is "ball" and a percent sign "balls."

The ampersand (&) can be translated to Latin and called "et."

"Star" is substituted for the three-syllable "asterisk" unless real stars are wanted.

The cents sign (¢) is usually just the letter *c*, "see" unless the actual symbol is requested. A dollar mark is "buck" and one of the most difficult things copyholders have to get used to is reading it ahead of the figures instead of the way they are accustomed to say it. It's "buck one" for $1—not one dollar. Read the last sentence aloud if you don't see why.

There are a number of styles for setting figures taken up later and the reader should note the one being used in the job so that it is not necessary to read more than the actual numbers. Usually a great many spoken syllables can be saved by saying each numeral by itself instead of using the combined forms—"one two one" for 121, not "one hun-dred and twen-ty-one."

Syllables can also be saved and accuracy increased by figuring out tabular matter and eliminating repetitions. It's almost always better to read tables down, rather than across.

Doubling of consonants should be shown by pronunciation if possible: "Phil-ip" or "Phil-lips." It can also be done by counting: "Phil-ip-pines—one and two," wherein the possibly doubled consonants are noted in order. The copyholder would not say "one and two" after *recommend* because the reader would be expected to know how to spell the word. He might do so after *Philippines* as a caustic observation that one writer had learned to spell the word.

Terminal doubling of consonants is usually shown by counting but *mann* and *man* occur frequently enough to use "mahn" for the former—unless the copyholder is Jamaican or otherwise unable to say "man."

Spanish is a wonderful language for copyholding. All of the vowels have a single pronunciation: *la* "law," *le* "lay," *li* "lee," *lo* "low," *lu* "loo." The system can be used for unfamiliar words in other languages.

Words ending in *y* nearly always need explanation. It takes a total mastery of spelling to dispense with it. In proper names there is no possibility of taking the spelling for granted. Thus if there is no *e* before the *y*, the word is pronounced normally:

"Shirly, whisky." If there is an *e* it should always be spoken—following the word: *Shirley* is "Shir-lee—E." *Whiskey* is "whiskee—E."

The *ei* and *ie* combinations are best rendered the German way, pronouncing the second letter only: *stein* is "stine" and *stien* is "steen." In the unusual event of such a word being spelled as pronounced, the spelling should be given: "stine, eye en ee."

Copyholding on normal revisions of proofs is an inefficient practice but some places require it because the boss likes to be sure everyone is busily at work. It can be useful if there is much re-running of paragraphs or lengthy inserts. In a revision the proof is "slugged." The first word of each line with no correction is read and when a correction appears the entire line is read as corrected—or as many lines as it was necessary to reset. This system can result in several kinds of errors that would have been spotted by a good proofreader revising by himself.

# 4

# Capitalization

A CHOICE INTERCHANGE in the musical "Lil Abner," which first appeared in the comic strip by Al Capp, comes when General Bullmoose attempts to secure the formula for the Yokumberry tonic.

BULLMOOSE: Yokum, my boy, it's time you and I talked a little business. I'm offering you a million dollars for the rights to your drug.

ABNER: But ah already told the President . . .

BULLMOOSE: President? What president?

ABNER: The President of the United States.

BULLMOOSE: Oh, that president!

You can practically hear the capitalization in the spoken words in that passage.

There being only one president of a country at any given time it is customary to capitalize the word when it means the office or the occupant of the office. The same goes for the president of a company or organization when the meaning is understood, as in their own publications or annual reports. There is a factor in publishing however that can change the circumstances. Magazines and newspapers operate under cover of datelines so that a "President" is personified as of the dateline. Other publications go on the shelves and outlast the occupants of offices.

The rules on capitalization of titles of office or nobility are broad and open to sometimes subtle considerations.

Titles are generally accorded capitalization in their own right provided that they are complete. The government printing office uses the rule: "To indicate pre-eminence or distinction in certain specified instances, a common-noun title immediately following the name of a person or used alone as a substitute for it is capitalized."

Note that they say "in specified instances." That brings it back to a matter of style and their style follows. So it will be with any publisher.

The office of Ambassador to France is a proper noun and used before or after the name of the person holding the office it becomes doubly so—as title and personification. Once established as personification the full title can be shortened and "the Ambassador" be considered to mean, say, Benjamin Franklin, Ambassador to France. Once the reference leaves the specific ambassadorship or the specific personification, however, there is opportunity to argue for or against capitalization of the word. The rank of Ambassador entitles its holder to immediate audience with the chief of state of the country to which he is Ambassador. If the meaning is the title it should be capitalized. If the meaning is simply one who represents another as an intermediary it is lower case—ambassador.

Coming down the line, the personification still holds to a degree but it isn't likely that a councilman or custodian will need to have his title capitalized even if a specific person is referred to, except when the title precedes the name in place of a given name or *Mr.*

Geographical references follow a simple enough rule for capitalization but still cause trouble. The generic explanations, like boulevard, street, river, county, bay, mountain and so forth are only capitalized when part of a proper name—Cook County,

Mississippi River, Nepotism Cliffs, etc. Newspapers drop the capital even in such cases. If a writer wishes to personify such references he may do so.

We know that the names of persons are capitalized but there is one aspect of this that a surprising number of editors do not understand. There is a firm rule on capitalization of the particles in proper names of persons: "A particle in a foreign name is only capitalized when not preceded by a given name, initials or title."

The most abused violation of this rule was, for a long time, in references to Charles de Gaulle, alias Gen. de Gaulle, Mr. De Gaulle, President de Gaulle or that so-and-so De Gaulle.

Another example that one can't read proof very long without encountering is the Du Pont Company or E. I. du Pont de Nemours & Co. That's the proper version although there seems to be some contradiction involved and there's a possibility that the Du Pont in this case is a given name, not the current family name. The company's labels and trade mark hedge with the name set in two words, all caps.

*D', da, della, du, van* and *von,* all translated "of," usually follow the above rule on capitalization. There are personal usage cases. The *GPO Style Manual* gives Samuel F. Du Pont and Irénée du Pont. Anglicized or American names do not necessarily follow the rule. In any case a surname should never be used alone, or with Mr., uncapitalized. That is, it cannot be so used correctly. If an editor wishes to flaunt his power to remain illiterate, the proofreader must bow to it.

The use of capitalization for pronouns referring to the Deity is supposed to be limited to cases where they are not closely linked to the proper noun, "God, in his wrath . . ." but some prefer that they always be capitalized.

Derivatives of proper nouns are sometimes up and sometimes down. The decision usually rests on whether the association is with the original name—Roman, but roman type; brussels sprouts, pasteurize, English language.

The points of the compass present a frequent problem in

capitalization. The rule is for capitalization where an area is identified, as in the Eastern Shore or the West Coast. If it's merely a direction, as, "west of here," lower case is used. Not all would go along with the recommended Northerner and Southerner.

The article *the* is capitalized only when it is actually a part of the proper name following it, if a proofreader has any way of knowing that. It can usually be presumed that *the* is a lower case article, especially in references to publications and ships. If a celtic chief is entitled to wear an eagle's feather he can be called "The."

The word following a colon is not necessarily capitalized. It is preferred that it not be if it is part of a clause supplementing the statement preceding the colon, even if it be a complete sentence.

There is no total logical approach to the capitalization of abbreviations. There is a rule that abbreviations should follow the capitalization of the word being abbreviated—which leaves the same gray area already noted for the spelled-out versions. There is a little-known drug labeling regulation that grams (Gm.) be capitalized to separate it as much as possible from grains (gr.) or a transposition to milligrams (mg.).

The metric system usually is represented by lower case abbreviations. Pounds, inches and ounces show up both ways. The new post office system of two-letter state abbreviations uses both letters in caps. This should be followed for direct envelope addresses but many prefer to stick to the old form for letterheads and text.

Which words in titles and other display matter should be capitalized? That's the most frequent problem for proofreaders since it's sometimes the reader's decision. Copy may be submitted in all capitals and marked to be set in caps and lower case.

The authorities all hedge a little on the rules for title capitalization. There is a consensus that nouns, pronouns, adjectives, adverbs, verbs and the first word of the title should be capitalized, although there is considerable tendency to make the word *is* lower case. One authority suggests capitalizing all words except "unemphatic" prepositions, conjunctions and articles. For the most part, general practice is to use lower case for those three classes if the words are three letters or less. Any word of four letters or more is then capitalized. There is a trend against capitalization in display lines in advertising and it is often dropped in titles in bibliographies.

There is no printing practice that is more subject to individual style rules than capitalization. If the rules are set down, the proofreader must learn them and even then keep a running check for inconsistency.

# 5

# Spelling

IT WOULDN'T BE proper to write a book on proofreading and copyediting without a chapter on spelling. One chapter isn't going to
add much to what you already know or need to know. You are
probably over the first level of learning to spell—otherwise you
wouldn't aspire to being a proofreader and would settle for something in the executive line.

The first level of learning to spell comes naturally to some
and is never achieved by others. It's simply soaking up what one
sees printed and retaining it in the memory. The second level is
the most difficult. It entails study of the rules of spelling. For that
you go to the orthography section of a dictionary. At the third, or
proofreader, level the stock spellings should be already mastered
and you are ready for the oddities and the references.

The one thing that a proofreader has the right, and duty, to
change from copy is an unapproved spelling. Even that is qualified
occasionally when it is the intent of the author to misspell a word.

The qualification that a spelling be unapproved makes spelling more difficult, for the dictionary writers don't dare buck in-
trenched illiteracy in spelling and too frequently have a bad spelling following the correct one. The proofreader must accept either

spelling, but store the information that a secondary spelling is being used, for the next time the word comes up.

Some of this secondary spelling is justifiable. Transition does exist. There is a continuing trend toward simpler spelling. But where a confusion of meaning is involved it's time to stop saying, "That's a good attempt. A lot of people spell it that way."

Take "forgo," which means to give up or sacrifice, and "forego," which means to precede. For each word the dictionaries give the other as an alternate spelling and woe betide the reader who even suggests the correct spelling for the particular meaning.

The British took a leap forward in 1969 and dropped the spellings "kerb" and "tyre." Their extra *u* has been nearly eliminated in the United States, save for *glamour*. Their *re* for *er* is frequent enough in the United States to make it an approved secondary spelling, especially in *theater*. In the provinces the local social arbiters don't care much about the quality of the performances so long as they are performed in "theatres." Though *theater* is spelled correctly in the educated sector there is still the necessity for the proofreader to check on proper nouns of specific theaters. The British "practise" of using *s* in place of *c* or *z* isn't "recognised" in the United States.

Secondary spellings become proliferated spellings in the case of people's names. Some examples have been shown in the chapter on copyholding. It is only during the last hundred years or so that much care has been exercised in spelling and that reference books have been available. Ancient records use every possible variation for the names of identical persons. When printing and the availability of references developed to the point where spellings were checked, whatever misspellings then current were frozen. It was just as well, for identification in a more populous world, to have added a multiplicity of family names derived from the limited ancestral originals available.

In the case of actors you can count on names having unusual spellings. Once a name has been registered with Actors' Equity no other actor is allowed to use it even though it is his own christened name. So the actor whose name is already registered must assume a new name or resort to a changed spelling.

A proofreader has many occasions to check references and sometimes must himself see to the proper arrangement of names in alphabetical order. He should be aware that there are different forms of indexing names.

The prefix *Mac* got shortened when the first American census was printed in full. To save space and type the printers made it a contraction—*M'*. Not having apostrophes they used inverted commas which showed up looking like superior *c*'s. Thus the spelling *Mc* and *Mc* developed. There is a myth that *Mc* is Irish and *Mac* is Scottish. Actually there are only *Macs* in both countries but once a birth is recorded as *Mc* the person becomes so named.

Encyclopedias and biographical dictionaries treat *Mc* as an abbreviation for purposes of indexing. A name beginning with *Mc* will be indexed just as though it was spelled *Mac*. Telephone directories and the current dictionaries that have dropped separate biographical and geographical sections, index according to literal spelling.

*Mac, D', de, del, du, van, von* and so forth mean "of" or "son of." Generally you will find the names beginning with *D* indexed in order, disregarding number of words or capitalization, in both the phone books and the dictionaries. The latter will occasionally invert a *de* and put the name under the specific family. The Count François de Grasse is under *G* but Charles de Gaulle is under *D*. Van and Von are usually inverted in dictionaries—Van Gogh is under *G*.

Another difference in indexing occurs in the case of two or more words. The space between words may be taken into account or ignored. In one system all of the names beginning with the separate word *van*, for instance, would be kept together. In the other a Vanderbilt would precede a Van Allen.

Trade-mark names are copyrighted spellings and have to be followed by an appropriate symbol to keep them that way—

($^R$) registered, ($^C$) copyright or ($^{TM}$) trade-mark. In addition to the symbol a footnote must appear stating the name of the owner of the trade-mark.

The word *fiberglass* is likely to turn up in any of six different spellings. The trade-mark spelling owned by Corning is *Fiberglas.* Pittsburgh Plate owns another version. When any trade-mark name is used in drug or fabric labeling or advertising it is required by law that the generic name follow the trade-mark name—Fiberglas, glass; Dacron, polyester; Helanca, nylon; Orlon, acrylic; and so forth.

Trade-marks fluctuate with time. A trade-mark for a product gets into the language on its own and eventually the courts decide it no longer belongs to the original owner. *Thermos* went that route after much litigation. Dictionaries carry disclaimers on trade-marks.

Rules for spelling are complex, full of exceptions, and any attempt to boil them down is sure to wind up containing errors. However, even unabridged dictionaries don't show all endings of words and a way of reasoning them out is helpful.

Adding a suffix may require the addition of a letter or the deletion of one. Either way, the purpose is to avoid confusion with another word or to follow pronunciation.

The word *sizable* is a good example of dropping the silent *e.* The *e* is needed in the root word *size* as it is in *force, base, trace* and so forth but is dropped—or should be—when suffixes are added unless there is conflict with another word. You can't turn dye into *dying* or singe into *singing.* If the *e* needs to be pronounced, as in *mileage, manageable* or *noticeable,* it is retained.

In proofreading the dropped *e* causes the most problems in *judgment* and *acknowledgment.* Most writers have learned to spell *judgment* but the other one is still a toss-up.

A *k* is added to words ending in *c* to make sure of the *k* pronunciation instead of an *s* one—*picnic, picnicking, picnicker.*

Doubling of consonants when suffixes are added is based on a pronunciation reasoning for the preferred spellings but to the proofroom it is a style choice. Newspapers rarely double them. The American Express uses "travelers" with its archaic "checques." *Travelers* is the preferred spelling. That is decided on the basis of the accent being on the first syllable. If the syllable preceding the suffix is accented it is usually preferred that the consonant be doubled—*preferred*.

The boom in suffixes for *program* brought on by computers led to the setting of *programmers, programming* but *programed* at first, following the pronunciation. Usage has defied that and now all the *m*'s are doubled.

Most printers use the jingle, *"I* before *e,* except after *c."* It works most of the time but not always—*seize, weird, their*.

The most frequently misspelled single word in printing is *complement*. That is because the department store copywriters almost unanimously believe that it is spelled *compliment*.

A pet peeve of readers is the non-word *warranteed*. "Warrantee" means one who receives a warranty. "Warrant" and "warranted" are the verb forms. Yet the expression "warranteed to" comes up in almost every tire advertisement. Some readers have speculated that it is a trick to nullify the warranty. This suspicion loses cognizance in face of the fact that most tire warranties are worthless anyway since they are based on fictitious list prices.

The commonly used but unique word *whiskey* is inadequately handled in many dictionaries, even unabridged ones. Bourbon or rye whiskey made in the United States is always spelled with an *e* but Scotch, Irish and even Canadian booze is "whisky." Most manufacturers observe these spellings carefully in their labeling and advertising. Even the dictionaries that mention this don't show the plurals. You can solve that problem by rules for the forming of plurals which are in the chapter on plurals.

In the United States there is no longer any such word as *towards,* but you will see it in print more often than the real word—*toward*.

On the graph measuring degrees of illiteracy, *toward* is the beginning point for the section labeled "well-educated." Another is *until*. *Until* and *till* are words in their own right. There's no reason for doing so but you can contract *until* to *'til* or even *till* to *til'* but the incorrect *'till* and *til* turn up frequently.

Likewise, there is a tendency to begin *round* with an apostrophe for no better reason than that the writer has seen it that way. *Round* is accepted as a substitute for *around* although each word has specific meanings of its own.

*Effect* and *affect* are strictly different words but continually incorrectly substituted for each other. The effect of this is to affect the meaning—not to effect it.

*Ensure* and *insure* also have different meanings but so many people think they are synonymous that they are so accepted. "Ensure" means to make sure something happens while "insure" is the verb referring to insurance against its happening. Admittedly, the preamble to the U.S. Constitution does say, ". . . to insure domestic tranquility . . ."

One would think that everyone knows the difference between *capital* and *capitol* but during the writing of this chapter two occasions of switching them occurred. The *ol* spelling is only for a building where legislators meet. Capital cities and capital funds are spelled *al*. In the capitals there are many businesses using the name and they may use either spelling.

There is no dictionary that will give you all of the kinds of spellings that need checking. Even proofrooms that are stocked with extensive references are frequently found wanting. Dictionaries are the prime source because they include word division. An atlas is useful for more extensive worldwide coverage.

For small United States cities the post office's *Zip Code Directory* gives complete national coverage but it's a good idea to collect maps of your area for the further breakdown of local streets and geographical names. New York readers may be surprised to discover that the only instance of the word "boro" is in connection with Brooklyn's Boro Hall. All the other great boroughs use the spelling meaning "small community."

The *World Almanac* is useful for the names of personalities, mainly actors, but it has some sports, political and musical notables. It also has a short version of the zip code directories.

Telephone directories are a necessity. The company will furnish outlying ones if requested.

The most difficult words to look up are wines and gourmet dishes and restaurateurs are notoriously careless with copy for menus. Book titles and authors are hard to find. The names of corporations aren't easy unless you have a broker who will give you a copy of *Standard and Poor's Stock Guide*.

To close the subject the following list contains the words used in the regional finals of a recent National Spelling Bee. Note that a careful pronunciation would give away the spelling of most of the words and looking for that is the best way to develop a spelling memory.

Lariat, pedagogic, fuchsia, whimsicality, hibernaculum, recrudescence, fallaciousness, aesthetic, bouillon, savant, notoriety, pirouette, tandem, cirrhosis, calypso, queue, ordnance, conchology, diphthong, accession, molybdenum, chaise, allemande, demoniac, papyrus, casserole, negligee, baccalaureate, eczema, stethoscope, phenomenon, etiquette, indefatigable, nomenclature, somnambulant, vacuum, ornithology, connoisseur, decorum, appendicitis, finesse, gubernatorial, yeomen, nubile, dischargeable, franchise, lenient, renaissance, entrepreneur, obsequious, xylophone, metamorphosis, omnibus, arthritis, putsch, hyssop, urbanism, aplomb, pagoda, dinosaur, shamrock, flagitious, juxtaposed, hierarchical, impecunious, pusillanimous, linoleum.

# 6

# Plurals, Possessives and Apostrophes

*"What we want are engineers and physicists."*

THE QUOTATION ABOVE, from a recruitment ad, caused some discussion in a New York proofroom. The reader handling the job didn't like the plural verb but two others thought it was all right without being able to analyze their reasons. The gentleman from Dixie said it would be done properly in the South—"what-all we want."

For most words the difference between forming the plural by adding *s* or *es* is determined by the need for an extra syllable in order to pronounce the word. Words ending in an *s*-sound need the *es*. If the word ends in a single *s* it is a style choice as to adding *ses*. *Buses* or *busses* is acceptable.

For words ending in *o* there are a variety of rules and exceptions for adding *s* or *es*. For proper nouns add *s* only.

For words ending in *i* the *s* alone is preferred. Variations from this usually come from misspelling the singular form. The word *alibi* has the plural *alibis*. The frequently incorrect *alibies* would be all right if the word was spelled *aliby* to begin with, under the next rule—that the plurals of words ending in *y* are formed by changing the *y* to *ies*. That goes for nouns or verbs—

*identity, identities, identify, identifies.* Again the rule does not apply to proper nouns.

An exception to this is a word ending in *ey.* The plural of *whiskey* is *whiskeys.* The plural of *whisky* is *whiskies.*

The plurals of words ending in *f, fe* or *ff* are sometimes formed by adding *s* and sometimes by the change to *ves: proofs* and *chiefs* but *wives* and *calves.* Somehow "the pounding hoofs" doesn't sound right but the dictionaries say it is.

The adopted Latin words are in transition. *Datum* and *data, phenomenon* and *phenomena* remain fixed in their Latin spellings but most words in common use have acquired the anglicized *s* plural.

Compound words usually add the *s* at the end, even if the result seems a little strange. *Teaspoonfuls* is official drug-labeling usage. The dictionaries give *sisters-in-law* but making that one possessive is open to discussion.

Abbreviations present several problems. There are those who maintain that there is no reason to make an abbreviation plural at all. To do so defeats the purpose of the abbreviation. However, the proofreader must live with the fact that in most copy plurals are added indiscriminately. At least they could avoid *lbs.* The plural of *libra* is *librae.*

One case where a plural abbreviation may clarify meaning is a situation in which two numbers are referred to with one abbreviation (between Fourth and Fifth Sts.). Using the plural abbreviation shows that both are streets, where one might be an avenue. Of course spelling out *streets* would be better.

Current use for plurals of capital letters or figures favors adding the *s* only—1970s, IQs. Some use an apostrophe, 1970's, IQ's. There are occasions where the apostrophe makes for clarity and occasions where it can be mistaken for a possessive. Both ways are acceptable.

Doubling of letters is used for the pluralization of some abbreviations, notably *pp.* for *pages.*

After getting the plural of the noun spelled right, the next step is to get the proper verb to go with it. Most writers can manage this if there are no complications in the syntax. Sometimes the sentence gets involved enough to make finding the subject noun a little difficult. When they begin with a singular noun like "one" and add "out of thousands and thousands of persons" or some such string of plurals they frequently pick up with a plural verb instead of holding to the true subject, which is singular.

The proofreader is on firm ground in spelling the verb correctly in such a case of a strayed subject but should use caution where there is any doubt about the intended subject. If the copy reads, "Our sources in Washington reports . . ." it's better to circle the noun and the verb and put a question mark in the margin.

Many proofreaders believe firmly that there are only plural and singular nouns. There is also a gray area composed of collective nouns which can be treated according to the wish of the writer—provided he doesn't get mixed up himself. The classic example is, "The committee finished its work and went to their homes." *Committee, group,* and even occasionally *United States* are among many words that can be used collectively. You may have questioned the use of "majority have" in the Foreword. It was correct usage because the author wanted to use it in the meaning of "largest number of persons." It would also have been correct to use "majority has" if he had meant one group as opposed to another group.

*Data* and *phenomena* are plural, a fact often forgotten by writers, but if a writer wants to think of some certain data as a particular mass of information there should be taken into account the possibility that he is using the word as a collective noun. Of course ambiguity can be avoided by using "collection of data" as it can be by "members of the committee."

A corporation is a single entity but in much informal writing one may be referred to in the plural and if the writer is consistent it isn't worth fighting over. The auto magazines usually refer to General Motors as "they."

Fractions need watching, for seven-eighths of something is singular while one and one-half objects are plural.

Plural nouns used as adjectives present problems. Consider the five-dollars bill. Everyone calls it a five-dollar bill and that is the proper way to refer to it.

But all such cases are not as easy. A ten-degrees temperature is apt to be preferred. In technical and formal writing the plural is preferred. Words dealing with time are preferred singular—24-hour day, 3-minute mile.

This leads into a controversial area. There is a tendency to make adjectives ending in *s* possessive. A majority will do it in the case of the three-week vacation. If the writer wishes to make the adjective plural it isn't irregular. Adding an apostrophe is wrong. If there were any good argument for doing so it would apply also to a one-week vacation. The proponents of the possessive would not be so apt to insist on "one-week's vacation."

Proper nouns are not so often victims of the unnecessary apostrophe but there is no controversy over it. There is a fixed name for a company, organization or periodical that must be learned or looked up.

The bankers aren't inclined to admit that anyone owns their banks but themselves—Manufacturers Hanover, Bankers Trust, The Merchants Bank.

Periodicals vary and not always logically. It's *Woman's Day, Parents' Magazine,* but *Reader's Digest* and *Publishers Weekly.*

People are inclined to refer to stores bearing their original proprietors' names with an added *s* which automatically infers the possessive. It's Gimbel's, Scott's, and Field's but The Emporium. R. H. Macy and Company set up a copyright form to deal with its name—Macy☆s. Sears ends with an *s* and the company's handling of the name is to use no apostrophe—Sears quality, all Sears stores.

Organizations usually don't make their names possessive of the words *club* and *association* but a few do. The Bakers, Butchers, Bartenders and Teamsters are some of the majority of labor organizations where there is no apostrophe preceding "Union." However, the Fishermen's, Laborers' and Ironworkers' Unions are examples of the other way. There are Woman's and Women's clubs.

Adding an *s* to either the word *men* or the word *women* can only be done legitimately in connection with an apostrophe but one of the burdens of proofreaders is that they must face the continued use of "mens suits" and "womens dresses." Ladies, girls and boys apparel can be tolerated. There is even one heavy advertiser in New York that insists on *mens* and *womens*.

The most difficult problem in the use of plurals and apostrophes is the case of the proper name that ends in an *s* or and *s* sound.

The answer to the choice of endings lies in the meaning involved and the way the word would be spoken. There is no absolute rule for the printed form.

The overall philosophical approach to the use of the apostrophe for possessives is as a contraction for the additional spoken *es* sound, used to the same purpose. It goes back to a manner of speaking that would have used "two-weekses vacation" if the intent was to make the word possessive. This has been changed to an agreed *'s* to show the possessive of a singular noun and an apostrophe only after the *s* in a plural noun.

Ordinarily the patterns of speech and writing are such that this suffices. The singular possessives of proper names present a choice. "Besses hat" could be written that way, as it would be spoken but there would be a stumbling by the reader as he looked for the apostrophe he is accustomed to see, so it is changed to "Bess's hat" in printing and the reader fills in the extra syllable himself. He also recognizes that there is only one Bess involved.

It gets stickier with plurals. What must be done is to show whether the word is singular or plural. "Paul Evans' house" is sufficient if it's his alone. To render a word explaining that it is the house of the Evans family it's necessary to show another syllable. Again you can deny the reader his apostrophe and write "the Paul Evanses house." That's unmistakably plural and possessive to anyone facing the fact of the apostrophe as a contraction. Using "the Paul Evans's house" is actually the same thing and a better way of printing it.

"For Jesus' sake" is the established preference for that phrase.

The pronouns, *his, her, their, your, our* and *whose* are possessive in themselves and don't take an apostrophe when an *s* is added. Some very good readers and writers slip up on some of these, particularly in the confusion with contractions. Even those who understand the usage perfectly are apt to get the wrong choice between *its* and *it's, whose* and *who's, theirs* and *there's.* It's advisable whenever one of those words appears to pause for a translation: it's (it is), who's (who is), there's (there is).

It's a different story with *one.* The pronoun isn't possessive itself but then neither is *it.* Very able writers are known to prefer "ones own wishes," making the pronoun possessive as opposed to *one's* meaning "one is." Norman Mailer on the other hand has a sentence containing, ". . . because one's able to feel one's way into . . ." He may have been hard put for something that would shock proofreaders.

Typographically, the apostrophe is in the same category as quotes. It is customary to adjust apostrophes in quality typography so that one isn't left hanging high and dry above vowels as in *e's.* It may also be advisable to do some shaving to fit it closer to the preceding letter or the *s.* In display lines it looks better if it is set a size smaller than the letters.

# 7

# Italics versus Quotes

NOVICE AND UNSCHOOLED writers use italics and quotes generously and indiscriminately. There are places where the two overlap and only a publishing professor would have the gall to set rules covering all cases.

There are certain rules, though, for the use of italics that are generally agreed upon and frequently violated. Setting up these rules wasn't an arbitrary thing that the rebellious should challenge as a matter of principle. Behind the rules is a need to show that certain words refer to a ship or a publication or some other named object that will be recognized from the context but wouldn't be if the majority of readers were not able, through the italics, to understand the significance of the words.

The names of ships and flying machines should always be italicized.

The names of works of art should always be italicized.

The names of publications—newspapers, periodicals and books—should always be italicized. This is of extreme importance, particularly in bibliographies, because the italics say that the italicized word is the name of a publication and can be referred to.

The lack of italics means it is not a publication—possibly a poem, play, publisher, author, article or something else.

The worst villains in the breakdown of this rule are the high-priced type designers, particularly those for the drug industry, who by their status can override the poor but qualified people.

The rule on publications only applies to a publication itself. The far-flung activities of some publishing companies are not included and at times it is hard to separate them. Time, Inc. publishes *Time,* and the New York News, Chicago Tribune Syndicate publishes the newspapers mentioned in the company name. The distinction gets a bit tighter in cases like the New York Times Neediest Cases Fund, sponsored by the *New York Times.* The name of a newspaper or periodical alone or with an identifying city name can be italicized. If the word "magazine" follows the name of one it should be italicized if it is capitalized, otherwise not.

The *New York Times* and some other publications in referring to themselves use caps and small caps. Most newspapers carry only bold face with their news faces and never use italics.

Formerly the names of motion pictures were always quoted as are short plays and poems unless referring to a published version of one. The movies have become the subject of so much serious criticism that they are now often granted the status of works of art and their titles italicized.

Foreign words and phrases should be italicized. The question arises, how popularized must a foreign word become among English-speaking people and still remain a foreign word? The answers that some believe in may be of importance to themselves but the purpose of the rule is only to point out that the words are foreign. *Also* is recognized as the German word if it's in italics.

It is proper to italicize those pseudo-Latin names for genera and species but the custom has fallen into disuse.

There are some common practices that are not rules. Published playscripts use italics for stage directions. Titles of corporation officers are usually set in italics (with the officers' names in caps and small caps). The same treatment is often given to business cards and letterheads.

Letters in mathematical expressions are usually italicized. They can be confused with abbreviations and signs. Our old friend $x$ could be misunderstood to be a times sign ($\times$). Actual abbreviations of one letter or "tan" for tangent are roman and it isn't unusual for there to be an n for number and another $n$ for an unknown, or other overlapping meanings.

The use of italics for emphasis is not controlled and our novices can be allowed to wallow in them. Used sparingly the practice has some value and is quite proper but it *tends* to insult the reader's *intelligence* and sound *homosexual.*

If italic type is used for purposes of emphasis, or just because the typographic designer wants a chunk of copy set that way, words that should be italicized are reversed to roman—unfailingly. This is expected of the printer.

Typesetting plants can provide italics for most typefaces. Sometimes it is necessary to do some finagling to mix italics with roman. There may be one font consisting of roman and italic and another of roman with bold. A job comes in requiring both italic and bold. That means setting the job in the roman with bold and when italics are wanted the font is switched and a duplicate line set that includes the italics. The two lines are sawed apart and the desired settings joined.

Sometimes italics are not available at all. In this case an underscore is proper, just as it is on the typewriter. Setting an underscore means taking a piece of rule the length of the type line and cutting away the unwanted parts of it. It must be substituted for an equal amount of leading. If the type is set solid it is unsuitable to do it by hand and it usually can be drawn better and quicker. Photo-composing machines can be persuaded to produce underscores if very talented operators work at it. Drawn or set, underscores should be set fairly close to the type, skipping the descenders.

One printing nicety that has been outlawed in certain quarters is the use of italic punctuation along with italicized words. It's one of those points, like putting periods and commas inside quotes, that good printers learn and editors usually don't. At the present state of the art it's necessary to find out what the particular publication's view is. Some of them are even demanding nothing but roman punctuation. It looks much better to have any punctuation adjoining an italicized word italicized.

The main overhang between italics and quotes is in the rule that words or letters referred to as words or letters should be italicized. Thus OHIO is a word with an *o* at each end. This is a clear-cut case of a word being referred to with no vestige of the meaning of the word involved. If a word is used in such a way as to have its meaning involved—as in a definition—it may be preferable to quote it. Some problem cases in the chapter on spelling can be used as examples. There are many borderline cases and one shouldn't be too quick to judge that either way is inappropriate.

A word used ironically is preferably quoted. "Ironically" isn't completely descriptive of the uses surrounding quoting of individual words and phrases. Usually the quotes infer an opposite meaning to what the word literally means—at least a different meaning. There's a need for such use in the uncredibility situation of so many sloganistic terms. It's the first thing a beginner must be broken of though.

We all know that direct quotations are quoted and that quotes within quotes are set with single quotes. Some British publishers have that the other way around. They also sometimes use a dash to begin a quotation. This is rare in the United States.

Quotation marks are omitted for quotations that are announced as such and set in smaller type or indented.

Misspellings and British spellings should usually be followed in direct quotations.

Quotation marks originally were not provided with type fonts. The compositor used apostrophes to close quotes and inverted commas to open them. This still occurs in handset jobs.

When quotation marks were added to type fonts they followed the appearance of the commas and apostrophes (" "). New faces often have opening quotes cut as such, with the bulge at the top. The typewriter uses one set for opening or closing and some typefaces have been cut that way. A few faces have been cut with only closing quotes which are used for both opening and closing quotations.

Quotation marks, periods and commas occupy more space than their color needs, giving an appearance of excessive space. Some maneuvering is usually necessary for a good typographic appearance. When the period or comma is used next to quotes the excess space is doubled. For this reason it is standard printing practice to put periods and commas inside of quotes. There are sufficient unqualified people monkeying with editing to make this a controversial problem for proofreaders.

The amateur editor, seeing a sentence ending with a period followed by quotation marks, comes to the correct deduction that logically the period should follow the quotes. He doesn't check up and find that in all good publishing the quotes are outside. If he is editing a manuscript that is typed correctly he proceeds to add transpose marks to put the periods outside. If the periods have been typed outside and the printer proceeds to set them inside, as should be done, our amateur orders them reset at the printer's expense. Most operators will follow copy even if it is inconsistent. Some will set it properly regardless of copy and some will confer with the proofroom before setting it.

Experienced readers will generally put the quotes outside even if the copy is wrong. If there is any inconsistency in copy the reader has the right to assume that standard setting is expected. In the case of copy that has been deliberately edited to put commas or periods outside of quotes he is on treacherous ground. The problem is whether the person doing the editing is going to be able to bull the job through or a professional is likely to overrule him. If the job is for any sort of responsible agency or publisher you can bet on the latter case. If it's for a one-man and "associates" agency or any other minor league player it may be the former.

The "Chicago" style manual, while still favoring quotes outside for direct quotations, has decided on putting commas and periods outside in connection with single words or phrases. This has been picked up by prestige publications but it will take years of struggle to impose it on the industry.

There are ligatures available placing the quotes directly above the period and the comma but they aren't often stocked or used.

In a continuous quote of two or more paragraphs, quotation marks are used only at the beginning of new paragraphs. This is easy to lose track of without a check-back and sometimes it's difficult to be sure where quotes are continuing but it is the reader's prerogative to eliminate quotes at the end of paragraphs where the quote continues into a new paragraph.

A centered head in quotes should be centered visually, not mechanically.

| "ETAOIN | | "ETAOIN |
| SHRDLU" | not | SHRDLU" |

In all display material of any quality the quotes are subject to maneuvering for optimum appearance. They may be lowered to the height of lower case letters, moved closer to the word, or set a size smaller than the words. Where hanging punctuation is specified quotes are not usually hung but one of them can be if that gives the appearance of a more balanced line.

# 8

# The Hyphen
# and the Dashes

ANYONE WHO HAS spent any time at all in proofreading will agree
that the hyphen and the dash are the most misused and mixed up
of all punctuation marks.

There is an unbelievable preponderance of writers, editors
and typists who don't understand the use of combined words and a
large percentage of them don't even appear to know the difference
between a hyphen and a dash—two exactly opposite punctuation
marks. Good secretaries are about the only class that can be de-
pended upon for proper usage.

The problem begins with the lack of a dash on the typewriter. Such an important item of punctuation should certainly
take precedence over several of the signs that are rarely used.
Typists can indicate a dash by using two hyphens. That is accepted by all qualified printers. There are many typists now using
a hyphen with a space on each side and usually it turns out
that it is their intention to show a dash. Printers are disinclined to
accept it as one and leave it to the proofroom to make the decision.

The hyphen is used to join words. Used at the end of a line,
it signals that the letters beginning the following line are a part of

one word. This joining hyphen is called the division hyphen. Before getting into the division hyphen the combination form needs considerable attention.

A stumbling block shared by many proofreaders is the belief that there is an unalterable law that each combined form is either one word or a hyphenated word—in all cases, now and forever.

Actually there is only a subtle distinction between a single word and a hyphenated word. There is absolutely no grammatical difference.

A dictionary will give a preference, as of the time it was printed, but it will qualify its decision with the kind of word it is and its meaning. Grammatically, a hyphenated word is one word. The distinction is that a hyphenated word is a temporary or transitional word. It is possible to combine any two or more words into a single word.

The rule for admitting a combination word into the language as a single word in its own right is that the new word have a separate meaning of its own, apart from the meaning of its original parts. A good example is the word *typewriter*.

type′writer *n.* One who operates a machine for the writing of characters similar to printers' types.

That still remains a secondary definition of the word. The point is that a typist or a machine called a typewriter is far enough removed from the words *type* and *writer* to become something else. Oddly we still call a machine for refrigerating and circulating air an "air conditioner."

That's the elementary part. There being no grammatical difference and only a slight possible difference in the meaning, hyphening or closing up a word can be left to the writer, the dictionary and conformity of usage—at least where nouns are concerned.

But the difference between two words and one word—whether the one word is really such or temporarily so, by being stuck together with a hyphen—is a little more complicated and can change a meaning completely.

As we can have temporary words, we can also consider the description of words as nouns, adjectives, verbs and so forth as a sometimes thing. Any word can be used as a noun equivalent. Just precede it with, "The word . . ." and you have a noun.

An adjective is a word that is used to describe a noun or another adjective. It makes no difference if the word itself is normally a verb or noun—a going concern, a can opener—it's all in how it is used.

Pressed for a justification for fitting odd sentence structures into parts-of-speech definitions, the experts classify whole phrases as nouns, adjectives and adverbs but that is aside from the practical use of hyphens.

In English, descriptive words march in order. Generally each word describes the word following it. You can put an adverb after a verb—moving slowly—but usually it's a case of a noun preceded by other words. If they aren't separated by commas or combined, each one applies to the word following it rather than to the eventual noun.

So we come to the trick of creating a temporary word in order to use it as a special kind of word.

Consider the strange case of the device for opening cans.

First you can eliminate proper nouns. There is an electricity-powered machine called the General Electric Can Opener. Since that is how it is christened or patented, that is the mandatory way to write it. The four capitalized words constitute one proper noun.

Then there is the wife whose husband claims to be of principal use as a can opener. *Can* is used as an adjective and *opener* as a noun. You can call her a can-opener if you need preceding adjectives that might be confused with *can*.

When it comes to one of the common devices designed for the sole purpose of opening cans, the term *can-opener* or *canopener* is indicated. The distinction is philosophical.

But what if you are referring to the finger-slashing device

built into cans or the pointed tube that's pounded into cans of oil and then used as a pouring spout?

In the case of the oil-can can-opener it is necessary to go back to using *opener* as a noun and to combine the other two nouns into a single adjective describing the noun. The result is an *oil-can opener.* An alternative is to create a conglomerate noun —*oil-can-opener.*

To expand the illustration a little more, let's say that you have just bought a good oil-can opener and paid too much for it —an expensive, newly purchased, well-made, oil-can opener.

The thing you are describing is the noun—*opener.*

*Expensive* is an adjective describing *opener.* It is followed by a comma to signal that it is describing the eventual noun, not the word following it.

*Newly,* however, is an adverb that is describing the word *purchased* so no hyphen is used.

*Well-made* is another case of an adverb-adjective combination and it is combined as an example of author's choice. When it seems to the writer that clarity is improved by combining an adverb and adjective it is his privilege to do so—not a proofreader's to tell him he mustn't. There is a great deal of querying and struggle between editors over the point—from which proofreaders should remain aloof.

Readers should be attentive particularly to the possibility of change of meaning in the case of derogatory words. Although *proofreader* is well established as a single word, suppose that one was reading a dirty proof. Even "dirty proof reader" would not suffice. It's necessary to get in there and establish what *dirty* applies to—a "dirty-proof reader."

Numbers that are printed as figures, abbreviations and symbols are treated exactly as though they were words. They follow the same rules for hyphening. Thus we say, "A 12-in. ruler is 12 inches in length." In the first part of the sentence "12-in." is an adjective combination describing the noun "ruler." In the last part, "12" is an adjective describing the noun "inches."

The same rule applies to those electronic manuals full of 12-VDC voltmeters, 12 V DC, 12-V DC-generators and other variations on 12 volts of direct current.

Or you might find: "Today's 90-degree temperature was 10 degrees higher than . . ."

Sometimes a single ending is used for two or more prefixes, usually numbers but occasionally words:

". . . 2-, 4- and 8-inch sizes."

". . . red-, white- and blue-colored poker chips."

Written numbers of two words and fractions are always joined with hyphens: thirty-two, one-third. That is one solid, unvariable rule any reader may invoke, regardless of copy. There is a possible difference of opinion on how numbers over one hundred should be handled. The bankers have agreed upon eliminating the word *and* in writing out the dollar amount. Checks should read "one hundred forty-six and no/100 dollars" rather than "one hundred and forty-six."

The use of hyphens in connection with prefixes is dependent upon ease of reading and avoidance of ambiguity. When a prefix is not a word itself, no hyphen is called for. When letters get doubled up or vowels combined in such a way as to mislead, it's more readable to use a hyphen—*re-elect, co-operate, re-issue.* There may be differing opinions in individual cases but clarity overrides other considerations.

In certain cases there is a consensus. Tripled letters in compounds require a hyphen—*cross-stroke.* Scientific combinations never use one—*microorganism.* Prefixes to proper nouns use it—*pro-Arab.*

Words like *bull's-eye* and *cat's-paw* must remain hyphened combinations because of the apostrophe even though the original elements have long been discarded.

There are instances where adding a prefix duplicates a word with a different meaning and the hyphen should be used to differentiate—"re-form" (to form again), "reform" (to mend one's ways).

*Word Division.*

Once upon a time proofreaders were the high priests of the division hyphen and the Merriam-Webster dictionaries, the *International* and its shortened version the *Collegiate,* their scripture. Readers took pride in the extent of their memory of the divisions revealed in this inspired work. When a copy became hopelessly worn out it was discreetly disposed of and a new, upnumbered volume replaced it. The new editions contained additional words but the word divisions remained steadfast.

Then, following the publication of the editions called *Third* and *Seventh,* there began appearing corrections from publishing houses and advertising agencies changing the division of *service* from *serv-ice* to *ser-vice* and the like. The corrections were sometimes accompanied by a note to "see Webster."

So the unthinkable was forced on the industry. Checking through the new dictionaries it became apparent that there had been wholesale changes in word divisions and all previous dictionaries were the victims of what appeared to be a planned obsolescence.

There had been scholarly criticism of the new, improved "Webster" in the press at the time of its publication but in the period of time before the division situation became commonly known it had taken hold.

Now we are engaged in a great civil controversy, testing whether the traditional word divisions shall remain or shall be replaced.

The chief rallying point for tradition is the distinguished Random House dictionary. The fine new American Heritage dictionary also swings its prestige to the banner of "serv-ice." Nero Wolfe ceremoniously burned his *Third,* page by page, and the editors of the *New York News* unceremoniously dumped their copies and replaced them with the Random House.

Most of the word-division books jumped on the Merriam-Webster bandwagon at the start, with some qualifications. In his latest editing of *50,000 Words*, Harry Sharp has reported both ways of dividing.

This corner prefers adherence to the traditional divisions unless a customer specifically orders using the *Third*. A good compromise position is the Government Printing Office's *Word Division*. In addition to its specific word breaks it has some sound rules and reasoning on formulating the breaks that every reader should learn.

The most troublesome word breaks are those of words beginning with *pro*. Actors and partly educated Americans use the affected emphasis on *pro* indiscriminately in speech and fail to recognize the meanings of the words. *Progress, produce* and *project* are dual words. Each can be either noun or verb and must be broken accordingly. The nouns are *prog-ress, prod-uce* and *proj-ect*. The verbs are *pro-gress, pro-duce* and *pro-ject*. The word *process* is both noun and verb and should always be broken *proc-ess*, according to the majority. "Webster" and the British say it should always be *pro-cess* but no educated American speaker would pronounce it that way.

Foreign word breaks must be accomplished by resorting to rules alone, there being no more dictionaries around that show divisions. Again the Chicago and GPO style manuals are the best sources for rules for division.

Spanish language printing is so common in the United States and its word division rules so uncomplicated that every reader should memorize them. Divide after a vowel or the first of two or more consonants is a good rule of thumb. Some would have it: divide before the last of two or more consonants. Either way, the rule is subject to keeping the following units intact: *bl, br, cl, cr, dr, fl, fr, gl, gr, pl, pr* and *tr*. There are three combinations of letters in Spanish that are regarded as single letters and must always begin a syllable intact: *ch, rr* and *ll*. Never begin a syllable with *s* and another consonant. There are a few vowel combinations that can be broken but they depend upon an understanding of the language.

In advertising typography it is taboo to break the name of the product or of the advertiser.

Telegraphing the probable balance of a broken word by breaking after its distinctive part is preferable. All rules are secondary to the requirements of good spacing—in impossible situations an improper break is permitted in preference to extremely bad spacing. This is particularly applicable to the rule against two-letter divisions.

Ragged lines are becoming almost as popular as justified lines and there is some disagreement on using word divisions in ragged matter. Most printers have been taught to use no divisions. This can get too shaggy for good appearance and readability. It also stretches copy depth. The best typography shops use hyphening as necessary to maintain a good contour. It is preferable to do so rather than to resort to uneven word space to obtain a good ragged right. If the type is set flush right and ragged left there is less reason for not breaking words.

At the time of writing, computer word division is crude and unsatisfactory but is in use. The newspapers assume that its faults are outweighed by the speed and simplification of typesetting. Computers divide by a combination of word storage and logic and divide correctly about half of the time. They don't come close on proper nouns.

A computer division can be corrected manually by the operator by resetting the line and ordering justification of the line at the correct point but in newspaper work this is only done for extremely bad division of extremely important material. In job work it must be done.

*The Dashes.*

To repeat, and it seems to need repeating, the em-dash (—) and the hyphen (-) are opposites. How many people editing copy there are who don't even know this is hard to estimate. There are too many. While this was being written, the copy chief of a major advertising agency struck down all attempts by the typesetters and the people in his agency to use a dash correctly and bulled a page ad for three New York newspapers into print with a hyphen that garbled the meaning.

There are other dashes besides the em-dash but the only one used as punctuation is the en-dash (–). This is shorter than the em-dash and is used primarily as a superhyphen. Its principal use is in joining two-word hookups. This is necessary to show that more than the words immediately adjoining an ordinary hyphen are being made part of the compound—a New York–Chicago flight for example. A hyphen there would mean, literally, a new flight between York and Chicago. While the meaning would be understandable a more complex compound would have its meaning changed.

The en-dash is also used as a substitute for "versus" and "between."

En-dashes aren't used often. They require extra effort by operators and aren't easily found in cases of hand type. When the typesetter does go to the trouble of inserting them, the usual editorial personnel aren't apt to recognize them and to call for hyphens instead.

The em-dash—which will now be referred to as the dash—is used to separate, rather than to join. It can be used as a substitute for the comma, parentheses, the colon or even the period. It's a very handy mark. It makes for greater readability and is great for adding a thought without having to go through the routine of a new formal sentence.

Some offices set up style rules for use of the dash as punctuation and for purposes other than punctuation.

Financial reports most frequently use two dashes to indicate blank amounts. (The Internal Revenue Service is advocating a single cipher in the dollar column for tax returns.)

Dashes can be cut to any length for special purposes but one em is standard for punctuation. In hand setting it is often necessary to cut a dash from a piece of rule. Make sure the dashes match each other and the hyphen.

There is an alternate dash available for machine setting called the ad-dash. This dash is a little shorter than its one-em body, allowing about one-half point of space on each side. It is only used when specified by the type designer. There is a difference of opinion among typographers as to whether it is desirable. Regular dashes sometimes butt against one letter and appear to have space between them and other, open, letters (l—T).

Except in dealing with stubborn rule makers, the proofreader should make judgments on the advisability to use space around regular dashes according to appearance in individual cases. It makes for a better looking line at times to maintain the type color by adding a point or two around dashes to balance with the spacing of the remainder of the line. Look out for this as an easy solution by the operator to a difficult justification problem.

The hyphen and the dash are positioned to center on the lower case vowels and when either is used between capitals in handset lines it should be raised to center on the capitals. Nothing can be done about it in machine setting.

# 9

# Commas, Colons
# and Semicolons

*Truly I say to you today you will be with me in paradise.*
—LUKE 23:43

THERE ARE TWO widely separated bodies of religious dogma based
on that quotation. The Revised Standard versions of the Bible put
a comma after the first *you*, but those who hold with the theory of
a purgatory and a one-shot judging of souls like the comma after
*today*.

This is an example of what the grammarians call the restric-
tive use of the comma. A word or phrase that can affect the meaning of the sentence is locked into its proper context.

Another example was heard on radio: "The bodies of the
woman and her daughter were found shot to death by the husband." Since there are no commas in the spoken language it will
remain a mystery where they belong and whether the husband
did the shooting or found the bodies.

Ordinarily the comma is a slight pause separating clauses,
phrases and words for grouping and ease of reading and doesn't
really affect meaning. Any style book will tell you that before
going into an extended set of rules for use of the comma.

There is enough tug-of-war between editors over commas
without the need for any help from the proofroom. The reader
should intervene only when the comma is meaningful or inconsistent with style.

This commentary on the comma is purposefully brief but the writing of it took more study and effort than most of the other chapters. The trouble with commas is that the deeper you delve into the rules in the dictionaries and style books, the more exceptions and contradictions you will find.

The title of this chapter illustrates one of the most common omissions of the comma. The most formal usage is to use one before a conjunction but it is eliminated in most writing. The previous sentence is another case study in the use of the comma before conjunctions. If the writer claims that the two independent clauses *are closely related* there is no need for a comma, otherwise (thiswise) a comma is required.

That sort of reasoning gets too complicated for a proofreader to add to his juggling repertoire of other forms of punctuation, spelling, capitalizing, type faces and so forth unless he has time to kill and wants to impress someone.

Even where there is no conjunction tying complete sentences together ("I came, I saw, I conquered.") it is still permissible to call the sentences clauses and separate them by commas instead of periods.

The inverted phrase is another example of use of the comma being only a style choice and a matter of judgment as to whether a particular sentence is easier to understand if a comma is added. If a writer wants to say "Four score and seven years ago our fathers brought forth upon this continent . . ." he doesn't have to apologize for turning a phrase by putting a comma after "ago" unless he wants to. Nero Wolfe's able secretary, Archie, prefers to begin sentences with prepositional phrases not followed by commas, which is an orderly way of thinking for reporters and detectives.

Few writers are able to get by with one adjective so commas are used after preliminary adjectives to signal that they apply to the upcoming noun rather than to the word following. It isn't necessary if the adjective preceding the noun is so closely related to the noun as to be a borderline case of becoming part of the noun—a large living room.

The parenthetical commas were formerly used in connection with dates and addresses appearing in sentences and are now being partially dropped, creating an anomaly which is excused by calling it an appositive.

Instead of October, 1971, the current practice is to write, "In October, 1971 your management . . ." It is the preferred style to use a full date with no commas if written with the inverted day date: "As of 31 December 1971 total assets were . . ."

The dropping of commas after the names of states or provinces, which was particularly parenthetical, is now a standard practice that creates the same anomaly. Using a comma between the name of a city and state has no logical excuse. It amounts to the same thing as using one between a given and surname. At the moment it is mandatory but will probably be phased out soon as needless to computer reading and addressing.

Addresses in one-line or text form require the comma after the normal breaks like name, company, street address, city and state. Envelope addressing eliminates the commas where new lines show the break. There should never be a comma between the state and the zip code.

There is rarely a case where copy for both letterheads (one line) and envelopes (three lines) is not supplied in one form or the other and the decision to supply or delete commas left to the printer. Most typesetters will follow copy literally and the commas must be added or deleted at the proof desk.

Commas before Inc., S.A., and so forth are a part of the mode of incorporation and, unless certain knowledge of the company usage exists, should follow copy.

The use of commas in direct quotations, as used in fiction, is best illustrated with examples.

"A complete sentence can end with a comma," she said.

"It can be interrupted," he said, "and continue."

"In a quotation, is it necessary to add a comma after a question mark?" she asked.

"Never!" he said.

The comma is now frequently dropped from four-figure numbers—1000 rather than 1,000. This is especially true of prices and of catalog and model numbers.

*The Colon and Semicolon.*

The permissiveness in allowing separate sentences to be joined into a single sentence extends to the semicolon. The semicolon is actually a supercomma that serves the same purpose and is primarily intended to add a degree more of separation when clauses separated by commas require their own interior commas. For instance: "Among those present were John Doe, New York; Peter Paul, Chicago; and Frank Corleone, Las Vegas."

There is evidence that there is confusion between the semicolon and the colon. The pair have nothing in common and the semicolon should never be used for any of the purposes for which the colon is used. Most likely this error in copy comes from forgetting to hit the shift key.

The colon should be used:

In a series that contains one or more complete sentences.

After "as follows" or "the following."

After introductory matter such as "Dear Sir," "Mr. Chairman," and the names of characters in play scripts. (It isn't necessary after "such as.")

In times, where hours and minutes are given—10:05.

After chapter numbers of the Bible—Luke 23:43.

In ratios—2:4::4:8.

Between the volume number and the page number in bibliographies. There are those who consider the volume number to be a part of the name of the publication and therefore to be italicized. This leads to the colon being subject to italicizing too, as punctuation following italicized matter should be. It's a minor point in itself but everything part of bibliography style is repeated so many times it must be consistent.

# 10

# Periods, Leaders and Bullets

THE ELEMENTARY USE of the period of course is to end a full sentence. That should require no elaboration but there is now an advertising practice of using incomplete sentences and even single words followed by periods. There is a corollary habit of using complete sentences without periods. Even some of the most formal publications, faced with the problem of lists containing both complete sentences and nonsentences, omit closing punctuation.

The sentence period should be followed by normal word space and, in a tight line, can have even less because the space above the period gives the appearance of there being extra space. Some British printers put a full em-quad between sentences.

The ellipsis is hardly ever used correctly in general printing. The ellipsis consists of three periods—not more nor less—with a little space between each and the adjoining words. It is used primarily to indicate a deletion in a quote. The other use is to separate short items. The columnists who use it for this purpose are the worst offenders in misuse.

*An ellipsis is used in addition to other punctuation.* Bad as the practice of using italics for emphasis is, that rule needs emphasizing.

If a complete sentence is followed by an ellipsis the regular period is used, closed up to the last word and then the ellipsis is added. The Random House dictionary uses four spaced periods in its example but that is not accepted practice.

If an ellipsis is used in midsentence only the ellipsis is used. There is usually no need for a comma in connection with an ellipsis but the author may want to show that one was used in the original being quoted.

In mathematics an ellipsis is used to show a sequence: 5, 10, . . . 40 means 5, 10, 15, 20, 25, 30, 35, 40.

Spacing around the periods that form an ellipsis should be uniform. There is disagreement as to whether the spacing of the entire line should be considered, rather than holding to a fixed amount of space. A standard amount is preferable but not if it results in excessive word space in the rest of the line.

Periods are sometimes used after abbreviations and sometimes not. Take note that the period is used after abbreviation of a word not a phrase. If a phrase like mph (miles per hour) is used no period is needed. In some cases each letter of such abbreviations is followed by a period.

There is no period used after symbols such as O for oxygen, Na for sodium, etc.

Contractions don't take periods.

There is a tendency, but far from a rule, to omit the period after metric system abbreviations while using it for other forms of measurements for weights and measures. On this point, however, proofreaders must keep a close watch for style on each word.

The most controversial period is the one that should not be used after the S in Harry S Truman. Mr. Truman constantly scolded the reporters for using it, explaining that the S is not an abbreviation for anything. The newspapers finally learned to omit the period. When his own daughter used it in her biography his supporters capitulated and the press and wire services used the period in his obituary.

The period is used as a decimal point in the U.S. and British countries but some countries reverse it with the comma, writing 1.000,00 for 1,000.00.

Constructed prices—a small dollar sign, a large dollar-amount figure, and a small cents-amount figure—never take the period, even though there is usually one in copy.

The British decimal system represents percentages of a pound. Thirty shillings is £1.50, there being twenty shillings in a pound.

In some instances the amount of space around the period can cause a typographically unattractive appearance that is to be avoided in good work. There are type refinements for letters such as the Y, in which the period is included with the letter for abbreviations such as N.Y. In handsetting or photosetting the period should be adjusted closer to the letter if excessive space appears.

The post office prefers two-letter, all-caps state abbreviations without periods.

Besides the regular periods of a font there are other dots with their own names and uses.

Leaders are lighter than the regular periods and are usually used leading into prices. They are included on the upper rail position of the em and en quads of linotype mats. Occasionally they will turn up unexpectedly in the midst of white space. Some typographers may prefer regular periods to leaders and in that case may specify period leaders. Of course there are also dash leaders, the opposing term being "period leaders." Confusing, what?

Leaders in tabular matter have a habit of becoming mis-aligned vertically. A reader should check for this.

· Centered dots are called bullets. Their main use is to introduce items in lists either as new paragraphs or run in. Keeping them centered is one of the proofreader's jobs because in hand setting they usually have to be built up to correspond to the size of the type they are being used with. Hand-type bullets come in most point sizes but on 6- and 12-point bodies.

· Linotype bullets come in most sizes of diameters. Since a one-point variation in size is difficult to identify, correction lines containing bullets often have the wrong size bullet.

· Any size of bullet can be produced by a photosetting machine. For practical purposes the Photon has two on the font negatives. The small one shows up as about two points in diameter on 12-pt type and the large one about four points. To get other sizes the magnification of the photo unit has to be switched.

· The size of the bullet in proportion to type size is a matter of personal taste. Some like them not much bigger than the periods and some want the full type size. The decision is often left to the printer. Those used here are 1½-point.

# 11

# Figures

A PROOFREADER DEALS with many kinds of numbers, not only the ones in copy. There are job numbers, galley numbers, location numbers, format numbers, and so on.

Proofreading figures is theoretically an idiot task requiring no knowledge and any mistake is the result of carelessness. You can't alibi a wrong figure. If the copy is not decipherable or subject to question it can be queried.

The greatest difficulty in reading figures is the similarity between the capital I, the lower case l, and the figure 1. The same situation exists between the capital O and the figure 0. The usual typewriter doesn't have a figure 1, but it is being included on the new machines. If no 1 is available the lower case l is supposed to be used but there are some who still use the I. The O and 0 are practically identical on typewriters and even in some typefaces.

In typefaces there is usually a distinctive figure 1. In most of the sans-serif faces it takes a skilled eye to recognize the difference between a 1 and an I. There may be only a slight difference in width. A few make the l slightly higher than the I. In the linotype Vogue there is actually a straight line for the Vogue Bold and a real figure 1 on the same mat for the extra bold.

When the telephone monopoly applied names to telephone exchanges they invented one of the biggest booby traps in printing and—for all their faults—they are to be praised for returning to pure numbers. Incidentally, the standard form for a number including an area code is (916) 371-1274. Some variations are still in use.

There are two sets of figures supplied with most of the old style faces. They are called "old style" and "lining" figures. Old style figures are cut like this: 1234567890 and lining figures: 1234567890.

Typographers, far from recognizing the possibility of confusion between letters and figures, are prone to choose the worst possible face for addresses and phone numbers. They also have made it fashionable to order that a capital I be substituted for the figure 1 in display lines.

Their avowed purpose in doing this is avoid excess space around the 1. Once in a while the dodge of substituting an I for a 1 will result in an improvement but usually it looks pretty bad.

Figures are generally cut in type on the same width body for each—one en—so that they will align in tabular matter. Teletypesetters have keys to provide 9 units of space (1 en).

Handwritten copy and editorial corrections add extra hazards for the proofreader. (See the chapter on marks.) One will frequently find a B substituted for 13, an S for an 8 or 5, and even more far-fetched deciphering of scribbles.

While the reader is not responsible for additions and other mathematical calculations it does no harm to at least keep an eye on them. It may turn up other errors. You may, for instance, be doing a financial statement where the sum is equal to less than any of its parts—due to a transposed rule. It's a good idea to take a second look at matter containing figures—wearing the hat of an interested consumer rather than a mindless checker. You may come upon a color TV set offered at $50 instead of $500—or a bank with assets of $3,000,000 instead of $3 billion.

The restrictions of the typewriter should be kept in mind in reading fractions. In order to write $1\frac{1}{16}$ on the typewriter it is necessary to write it with either a space or hyphen between the whole figure and the fraction (1-1/16). Otherwise it would read $1\frac{1}{16}$. It's up to the copyeditor, typesetter or proofreader to eliminate this space or hyphen if a piece (or "case") fraction has been used ($1\frac{1}{16}$). Type fractions are available in a wide variety and can be made up by hand or photosetting for any fraction. Occasionally a fraction will be called for, using full figures and a slant and only in that case should there be a hyphen or—if incorrectly insisted upon—a space, between the figure and fraction. (See the chapter on hyphens and dashes for the use of the hyphen with figures.)

There is a generally accepted rule for the setting of dollar amounts in newspaper advertising. A round figure in dollars is set with dollar mark and no period or ciphers ($5). For a dollar and cents figure the dollar mark is eliminated (4.98). A few advertisers depart from this but for the great bulk of copy the above style is used. Newspaper advertising copy as a rule is so filled with inconsistencies that it is necessary to proceed by a general style, disregarding copy. The general rule for display prices is to set the $ sign and the digits representing cents one-half the size of the digits representing dollars.

In other matter the reader should search out the desired style when prices first appear. If it's a job of any considerable size, such as a catalog, he should confer with others working on the job, not only on the dollar handling but on typefaces, positioning of prices (they usually are set flush right, with leaders), method of aligning and anything else subject to more than one style of setting.

All readers should make an attempt to verify zip codes and get them included in addresses. Even some of our biggest corporations continue to blithely print coupons and stationery without bothering to supply their zip code. The typesetters' readers can only suggest inclusion if there is no zip code but if one has the postal zip code directory or can obtain the number from the telephone directory he should check the number supplied and correct it if necessary.

Advertisers use a code for reply mail to ascertain the response from each publication in which they advertise. Sometimes it's a box number following the name of the company and sometimes it's a number inserted in very small type at the bottom of a coupon. Usually you can decode it. NYT-872 probably would mean: *New York Times* inserted August, 1972. Wherever such a number occurs there are usually other settings for other publications or editions. Sometimes only the numbers are set and proofed for pasting into the art work. Sometimes the entire paragraph containing the address is set for each change. Newspapers often saw the numbers out of plates and set the one supplied with the copy in the nearest face they have and mortise it into the plate.

Superior figures usually mean powers of the number or refer to footnotes. Inferior figures are sometimes called valance figures because they are used to denote the number of atoms of an element contained in a molecule.

The figures denoting the number of various lettered vitamins are set in different ways. There is no necessity for using an inferior figure except to save space. The number is part of the name. Riboflavin is Vitamin B number 2 (B-2) but if they want it set $B_2$ that's acceptable if consistent.

Most typesetting shops carry magnetic numbers, a good thing to keep in mind in connection with your own checking account, for these numbers printed at the bottom of your checks constitute your signature. On a check, magnetic figures tell the number of the bank and the number of the account. They are printed with a magnetic ink that can be read by a computer. They come in one size only and spacing is of no importance.

There are identifying numbers on proofs that are not for printing but can be as important as the part that is. A typesetting shop usually includes its own job number, the name of the customer ordering the job with either, or both, the customer's job number and purchase order number, and for an agency its client's job number, for multiple galleys, the galley number. There is usually an identification of the stage of revision as FP (first proof), 1R (1st revise), etc., and the date of delivery or setting or revising of the job.

Advertising agencies usually have their own set of guidelines —called taglines. Each has its own style but they generally include advertisement number, job number and dates of publication.

Newspapers have sluglines. They identify the head for news stories and the take number. News stories are usually cut up into small units so that a single story can be set simultaneously by several operators. The floorman puts the takes together by these numbers.

Other numbers used for identification on newspapers include insertion dates and lineage and column identification.

Book work carries considerable bookkeeping problems for the reader. A typical textbook will have type-sizes and measures for the main text, for examples and for footnotes. It will have illustrations and tables to be inserted at the proper places. It will usually be done by chapters and fed to the publisher in galleys as completed. Then alterations will be made and the pages will be made up. All of this requires a control system showing what pages of manuscript have become what galleys and what galleys have become what pages, where they are at any particular time and where the type, negatives or art is located. The typesetter's reader carries notes on the galleys of illustrations and tables and footnotes that are to be inserted.

Packaging requires coding running through each size and potency of each unit including primary labels, cartons, shipping cases and so forth. In addition there are usually batch numbers, export versions and license numbers.

# 12

# The Query and the Crystal Ball

HAVING TO CONSULT the crystal ball is mentioned frequently in proofrooms for it is a rare piece of copy that doesn't contain something suspect, contradictory or unintelligible.

The discounters of psychic phenomena explain the working of the crystal ball as an unfocusing of the conscious mind wherein staring into the ball allows the mind to make a free search of unconsciously remembered data and to organize it into a summed-up revelation. It might work but it would be advisable to try it on your own time.

Requesting a decision on something in copy that seems wrong can also be accomplished by querying and there are times when that is the best or only way.

Before getting into how and whom to query, though, there should be some consideration of the possibility of avoiding the query. There are important reasons for doing so. There may not be enough time to go through the process of getting a decision and to have the job corrected and revised. This is true on newspapers and in urgent job work. There is also the reader's reputation as a person of intelligence and good judgment. And there is to be kept in mind the fact that a query usually is a suggestion that someone has made a mistake. Whoever that is will not likely feel properly grateful toward the person who discovers his error— if it is an error. He will feel righteous indignation if his copy was correct. Under no circumstances should a query be allowed to sound sarcastic or critical.

On clear-cut misspellings, as has been mentioned, it's the reader's job to make the correction and there is usually no need to query the copy additionally. There are instances of capitalization and punctuation that can be corrected at the proofdesk. Don't misunderstand this. It is only a general approach. In some work it is absolutely taboo to make any changes from copy or to make them without clear notice that copy was not followed.

A true case of making a necessary correction without fuss deserves recording. It isn't at all unique. A typesetter's reader working on a motel directory received copy with Albuquerque spelled *Albukerque* and corrected it on his proof. Back came the proof from the agency with the correct spelling changed to *Albuquerkee.* A second reader, who believed in following copy out the window, let them have their way and sent the proof out misspelled as ordered. This time the agency returned the proof corrected back to *Albukerque.* When a third shop reader again returned it to the correct spelling the agency gave up attempting to misspell the word.

It is this kind of experience, often repeated, that turns readers into constant queriers.

One of the most efficient ways of avoiding queries and at the same time assuring that the customer gets the message and does not suffer delay waiting for the correction is the alternate setting. A shop reader, spotting a probable error, can order a patch to be set as he believes the copy should read and proofed outside the setting with the possible error. Or he may wish to have his correction inserted and the copy version set off from the body of the job. This is called "hanging" or "floating." The proof correction is the regular marking plus the notation, "Set and hang." Or, "Hang old setting."

Good operators often set an alternate line on their own initiative and leave the big decision of which line to kill or hang to the reader. It saves sending the job back to the machine and points out an error that the reader might miss.

A frequent dilemma is the line that doesn't fit. Sometimes an alternate line is set, taking liberties with the copy, such as abbreviations or figures or changing type size or face. A display line that doesn't fit a layout may not have been intended to but been specified with the intention of making it the exact size wanted on camera. That way there is no need to compromise on typographic quality. In cases where that intention is not made clear a line may be added reading, "Set for reduction" or "Set for blowup."

Avoiding petty queries is admirable but a decision on what is too petty to query requires a top degree of intelligence and information. It varies with every kind of job. The promotion departments of major publishers sometimes perpetrate crimes against the language that would not get by the typists for the companies' books. The average department store or trade products advertiser doesn't care at all about punctuation, capitalization or sentence structure so long as the price is right and there are plenty of exclamation points. Proofreaders of limited ability are apt to do more querying than those who could cut up the most pretentious writing.

The expense involved in making corrections is a factor to be considered in corrections versus queries. That is the primary purpose of the chapter on printing economics. A direct typographical error is supposed to be corrected with the time involved in making it followed by a no-charge notation on the time cards of the men making the correction. Authors' alterations being charged for at double the regular rate, make any considerable correction of copy mistakes costly to the typesetter. The foreman may have different ideas than the reader on whether to make corrections that are the customer's fault.

The standard form of query, as given in the chapter of proofreader's marks, is the suggested correction followed by a slant and a question mark and circled. The person who answers the query should either strike out the whole query or the question mark.

There is no standard procedure for forwarding queries. Sometimes it is done on the typesetter's copy. The typesetter's reader can put queries on his proofs but there is no guarantee that they will ever get to anyone for whom they are intended. Some shops forbid making any queries on copy. On textbooks even the editors confine themselves to pasting tabs to the copy with their queries. The nearest thing to a standard system is the one of one set of proofs being selected for carrying queries and designated "Master Set." This requires an intermediary arrangement between the various readers and the master proof.

There has always been the problem of several sets of proofs with their different corrections and queries but with the proliferation of duplicating machines there are now apt to be several sets of copy.

The standard query can be given a different twist by the proofreader answering his own query. This has some good uses but should be approached with caution. Don't be sneaky about it —making it appear that someone else has taken the responsibility. One advantage is timing. In proofreading a job of length there will be possible errors that may be cleared up later in the text or may be forgotten if temporarily passed over. Thus a temporary query is made pending a possible solution. Another advantage is that there is a record of the departure from copy or that the copy was followed with reservations. For the many instances of minor illiteracies that the reader doesn't intend to correct or query a small check mark may be useful as a record that copy was followed though not approved of.

The hedging query has its uses. To make a hedging query the reader just writes OK? in the margin instead of a suggested change. The meaning of the OK? query may be that the reader wants verification that the setting is acceptable as the least objectionable one. It may mean that there is something definitely wrong that the author, editor or typographer must supply the remedy to but that the reader cannot.

An example of the last situation is the singular subject and the plural verb or vice versa where the one or the other needs changing but the reader can't make the recommendation for lack of information. Or the reader may note an error in addition. He has no way of knowing whether the sum or the parts are at fault so he queries the total "OK?"

In circumstances where the reader is strictly bound to follow copy the OK? is used to denote a proofreader's correction for as simple a matter as a corrected spelling. After the spelling has been corrected he may query the proof "OK? MS Page . . ."

The hunger for praise often leads to the verbal query. A reader trots to his nearest superior with a catch he has made and is told to let it go or change it. Instead of a pat on the head he may wind up holding the bag on missing or perpetrating an error. There are times when conferences are advisable but the written query is safer. Corrections made from telephone instructions should carry memoranda that they were such and from whom.

On queries concerning style the reader should refer to the location of different usage.

A form of query that crops up occasionally is "No copy?" This is usually a disclaimer by the reader for something on the proof that there is no copy for, or for a job he is asked to "scan" for typos only. It can be that there is no copy for the very good reason that something has been inserted that should not have been—like a Gimbels logo in a Macy ad. It happens.

The first proof pulled in a trade plant goes to the typesetter's reader. If he is permitted by house policy to do so he will put queries on the copy but usually he puts them on the proof. The proof goes to the desk of the foreman who can strike out the queries—or any outright corrections for that matter. He can authorize making the suggested correction or can mark it "carry" meaning that it is to go on one of the customer's proofs.

If you have read well the previous chapters of this book you should know more about matters that are apt to be wrong than ninety-some per cent of trade-plant foremen. They are selected from the printers on a basis of skill and energy on the job combined with that undefinable quality that fills the casting requirements for the part. You should rate well above editorial help in publishing and newspapers too but that's a jurisdictional problem.

Even if a foreman is as qualified as the reader he still hasn't studied a particular piece of copy as carefully and may miss a query raised from a point of style or previous instructions. He is also more interested in getting the job out on time. Conflicts develop.

There is no easy way of resolving these conflicts. If a foreman strikes out a correction or a query the reader has some options. He can let it drop. He can take the proof to the foreman and protest. He can carry the marks to succeeding proofs.

Letting it drop is best in some borderline cases. Theoretically, once a query or correction has been made on the first reading the reader is no longer responsible. That doesn't take into account the fact that one shift can contain quite a lot of printed words. Management can only check back on the occasional bad errors. Dirty proofs will be thought of as bad proofreading.

Arguing with the foreman may wear him down against future arbitrary acts and it may be possible to explain the necessity for a query or correction that he has misunderstood. In that case he gets saved from the blame for his worst blunders.

Making the correction or query again on the next proof amounts to acknowledging a state of war. It may as well be acknowledged if it exists. If an arrogant foreman makes a practice of thinning out corrections his readers cannot operate efficiently. The good ones take a minute to explain their reasons for overruling readers.

Some queries are by their nature addressed to the foreman, particularly in shops where the foremen double as markup men for jobs coming in without specific setting instructions. Queries can be addressed so that the intent to carry them is shown as "Ed." for editor, "Client," "Author" and so forth.

Proofreaders in editorial or agency situations may have problems similar to the printers' readers and their foremen, but the opportunity usually exists to go over the heads of intervening minor editors and at the fountainhead of the word business a little more respect is given to the content of the product than in the metal, ink and photo factories.

This is an appropriate place to mention legal restrictions. Although proofreaders in normal circumstances shouldn't try to act as legal counsel to copy desks they can sometimes make useful queries.

The broadest form of restriction on advertising is that a product should not be represented to be something it is not. Advertising people are incorrigibly persuaded that it is their duty to exaggerate the merits of products—at least as far as they can get away with outside of downright misrepresentation. There are no cops lying in wait to pounce upon violators of most laws on advertising. There is the chance that a competitor may complain if an ad is too far out of line. Unqualified use of *best* is apt to draw fire.

It is fraudulent to advertise a product as something it is not. A gold bracelet must be made of real gold. If it is only gold colored it must be so referred to. That goes for all precious metals. Diamond jewelry advertised as of certain carat weight must state whether the weight is total or of individual stones. A collection of chip diamonds weighing one-half carat is less valuable than a single half-carat diamond. Incidentally, jewelers use *ct.* for carats in stones and *kt.* for gold.

The furniture people are supposed to be talking about solid hardwoods when they say something is cherry, maple or mahogany. Otherwise they should add "veneer" or "trim."

In New York there is a specific law against using a fictitious price from which an article is supposed to have been reduced.

Other states have similar laws. An advertiser is supposed to be able to prove that the article was actually sold at the claimed price if "formerly," "originally" or "reduced from" is used. The compromise "comparable to" has been accepted.

Fabrics are supposed to be labeled and advertised exactly as to content although even Sears may omit this occasionally. The generic name must follow immediately the trademark name as Orlon acrylic, Helanca nylon, Dacron polyester, Fiberglas glass.

Drug labeling and advertising is subject to much stricter enforcement and most of the trickery is in the consumer's carelessness or inability to evaluate claims.

The Food and Drug Administration rides herd on the drug manufacturers not so much from great bureaucratic power as from the fact that without its approval or against its orders the companies would be subject to very damaging legal actions.

Names of drug products in both labeling and advertising must be followed by generic names in type of equal size. If a vitamin is not of proven usefulness, note must be made of the fact. That rule may be extended to entire patented products. There are standard lines that must be included when appropriate such as "May be habit-forming," and "Use only upon prescription of a physician." Any other cautions and warnings demanded by the FDA must be included.

The caution on cigarettes is well known.

Copyright infringement and libel are specialist areas but accusation of guilt in criminal cases should be checked to see that they are quoting the accuser or qualified by "alleged." Editors are usually on hand on newspapers to be queried in person on this one. Police reporters tend to get overanxious to convict arrested persons, sometimes winding up with massive libel suits against their publishers.

# 13

# Measuring

THE CHAPTER FOLLOWING this one will go into the ways that type is set and spaced. This one is about the measurements that are specified, and ways of checking them. Many readers never get the hang of this part of their work.

Everything having to do with type is measured in the pica system. Paper sizes and some kinds of type areas are measured in inches. The thickness of paper is measured in weight in pounds of 500 sheets of standard sizes—which is only incidental information for most readers.

There is an approximate relationship between picas and inches of six picas to the inch. This is inaccurate to the amount that 42 picas is $6^{15}/_{16}$ inches instead of seven inches.

A pica is divided into twelve points. Below that there is spacing material in sizes of $\frac{1}{2}$ point and $\frac{1}{4}$ point.

There are metal rules in $\frac{1}{2}$ point and hairline and most of the full range of point sizes. For paste makeup drafting tape is used. It comes in fractions of an inch and point sizes must be approximated.

When it is necessary to convert specifications in inches to points and picas there is often a need for approximation. If specifications are given in inches the printer must make the conversion. It helps if the measures are specified in the pica system because the specifier or office reader is in better position to know what tolerance is required. Fractions of inches are particularly difficult to work with. An eighth of an inch is 1½ points which is too fine a tolerance for most purposes. At the dimension of one point the eye begins to play tricks and measuring with a pica gauge is impractical. (*Gage* is the preferred technical spelling but it may be controversial here.) A difference of one point in the leading between lines is detectable by eye if the total leading is small. It takes a good eye to spot two-point leading among a number of lines having three-point leading.

The thickness of a rule is more apparent. A one-point rule shows up rather black and even a ½-point rule or hairline is identifiable if the proof is good. One point more or less between letters may be unnoticeable or very much noticeable, depending on the type size and such things as adjoining letters with vertical sides.

These fine measurements must usually be made by comparison with samples known to be correct. For most measuring, the pica gauge with its broader increments is used. Gauges showing one-point increments are rare. They usually show picas and half picas which are sufficient as will be shown later. In addition to pica measurements a gauge should also have inches and agate lines. Agate is a type size with a direct relationship to inches. It is ¼₄ inch or about 5½ points. Agate is used for classified, box scores and market reports but the measurement itself is used for charging for newspaper space even up to full page depths so a gauge is necessary to find depths.

A pica gauge is a necessity for a proofreader and being in limited demand may not be easily obtainable. There is usually someone who specializes in selling gauges and other tools to the printers in a city and can be contacted by inquiring of them. Any graphic arts supply house can at least order one. Art-supply stores usually stock only the plastic ones with an assortment of type sizes that is unnecessary once you have learned to use the pica gauge properly. A steel gauge is preferable.

There are two measurements that must be made on all jobs: length of lines and type size plus leading. Anyone can measure line length but only a small percentage of readers know how to check the other.

Type size cannot be measured on a proof with a gauge. It can only be done accurately by comparison with type samples. Type size is the depth of the body on which all characters of the font are cast. Few characters occupy the entire body. Usually the type size is the same as the distance from the top of the capitals to the bottoms of the descenders.

There are all kinds of exceptions to this even if you have a convenient *Iy* to measure. Some faces don't use the full body of the type at all. There are alternate long-descender characters for the y, p, q, j, and g that may go beyond the depth of the given type size, making it necessary to set 12-pt. type on a 13-pt. body. In many faces there are two sizes of type using the same body. These are specified by point size plus "small" or "large" or some other designation. Copperplate Gothic and Liteline Gothic come in four sizes of six-point and four sizes of twelve-point and are identified by numbers 1 to 4.

There are differences even in identically specified types. One of the trickiest is machine-set Optima. There is one Optima with roman and italic on the same mat and another with roman and boldface on the same mat. The 10-pt. Optima with bold has about the same character size as the 12-pt. Optima with italic.

So many variations exist that the use of a type specimen book is necessary for absolute identification of size but with enough experience and other points of reference a reader can verify sizes accurately most of the time without a book.

The key point of reference is the sum of the type size plus the line leading. This can be determined accurately by measuring.

The word "lead" has many meanings. In typesetting a lead is a piece of spacing material two points thick. However, the verb "lead" means to insert a given number of points of spacing material between lines of type. The amount is usually specified in even points but half-point material can be used. There is what amounts to minus leading. This can be created by cutting the base of the type off or in photosetting by advancing the paper less than the type size.

Leading on linotype work can be done by casting the type on a larger body or it can be done by setting the body the same size as the face and inserting space by hand. As there is no way to tell which kind of leading was used by looking at the proof, correction lines often get inserted without leading or with too much.

Most readers go along in a hit-or-miss way of trying to estimate leading plus type size by some device or other—trusting to the eye for the space between lines or trying to find a place on their multiple-point-size gauges where the proof lines line up.

There is an accurate, easy way to measure for the sum of the type size and leading but it takes a little practice. Measure the depth of three lines and divide by three. In a short time it can be done instantly. Try it on this page. Take any four lines and measure from the base of one to the base of the third line below it. This type is 10-point, leaded 3 points, or 10 on 13. You will find that three lines measure three picas plus half-way between the three-pica mark and the next half-pica mark. The total depth is three picas plus three points—39 points. Division by three gives 13 points.

Three lines of any even-numbered point size strike exactly on the pica or half-pica marks. Three lines of 8-point type come to two picas; three lines of 10-point make two and one-half picas. An odd number of points will strike just half-way between marks as in the example.

Once this solid reference point of the sum is established, the estimation of leading in proportion to type size can be more safely transferred to the eye.

Visual space is sometimes specified. This can be measured

between all-capital lines but needs to be averaged in mixed lines because the ascenders and descenders break up the apparent space between the x-height letters. In predominantly lower case lines the distance between the base of the line above to the top of the lower case vowels may be considered the visual space.

The fact that some type-faces must be set on a one-point larger body than the type size raises some controversy among printers. If, for instance, the specifications call for our friend 10-point Optima Medium with two-point leading there are two possibilities. The markup may mean ten on twelve. There is also some argument for reasoning that the normal body being eleven points deep, the two points of leading make it ten on thirteen. The proofroom ruling should be that the specifications call for two points total leading and the combination used to achieve it is not a factor to the customer. Therefore the sum should be ten on twelve. If the type specifier knows his job he will write 10/12 or 10/13 to begin with and there will be no reason for misunderstanding.

There is a more difficult problem where type is specified 10/12 with four points of paragraph spacing. Taken literally this would mean two points *additional* paragraph leading (10/14). Usually it is interpreted as four points additional or 10/16.

While checking the width of the type line, or "measure," doesn't call for any special skill, typesetting machines may have an error factor of one point and this isn't important except when correction lines are set on a different machine than the one used for the original setting. One point too little or too much shows up enough in a margin to make resetting necessary and should be marked. An exactly same-length line can also be positioned, so that it shows out of line on both margins. This can be corrected by hand if marked to align.

There are jobs where several kinds of widths within a line are involved—tabular or different amounts of indentions—and it is sometimes helpful to rule the proof with vertical lines setting off the areas to be checked. This can confuse the printers and should be done with a fine-point pen of a different color than the one used for corrections. Even in ragged matter it is sometimes helpful to draw a line showing the maximum width, for calculation of amount of raggedness and whether it can be improved.

Final proofs are checked on a lineup table—a lighted board with movable markers. The proof is positioned so that the lines are true and the margins and any other points that might be out of line, or not square, are ruled.

Tabular matter requires a series of measures in one line and can be set in individual column pieces or with individual lines butted to make the full line. It helps to know which way was used but if the reader doesn't know he must check the entire line for alignment and new errors when reading a correction line.

Typewriters advance paper one pica per line. This fact is often ignored in making up forms that are to be filled in by typewriter, but forms should be spaced so that areas to be filled in fall in even picas apart. If "typewriter spacing" is specified, it must be done.

Just as two angles of a triangle make the third angle mandatory, the leaded type size and measure determine the depth of a type area. The typographer works from a given area and tries to specify type size and leading to fit it. A lot of scheming has been done to provide foolproof systems of type casting. Rarely does any system work exactly and it becomes necessary to make some kind of adjustment to fit.

The easiest way to increase depth to fill an area or a page or to balance columns is to add spacing between lines. It is completely unacceptable to do this unevenly. Any addition of line spacing must apply to the entire job except in rare cases on newspapers when a single paragraph is leaded out.

There is more tolerance of leading between paragraphs—too much more. This is unacceptable in good advertising typography or book work but is accepted in some forms of work that are mostly informational rather than impressive. There are even third-echelon typographers who prefer some extra space between paragraphs. A job having facing pages or balanced columns looks amateurish if there are more paragraphs on one side than the other—making it necessary to increase spacing on the side with the least number of paragraphs.

To avoid this, a single odd line is sometimes picked up by rerunning part of a paragraph to shorten or lengthen it by one line. In some kinds of work a tolerance is allowed in page depth so that facing pages are kept to equal depths. This solution is used by computers assigned to make up an entire book. In book work and quality printing jobs the pages are made up to layout specifications and excess lines are hung outside of the made-up areas for editing. Between galley proofs and page makeup, copy-editors should make corrections that will allow for fit.

Newspapers using photosetting must of necessity cut apart the phototype to fill areas allotted to news stories or have makeup editors okay the cutting away of some of the type.

There are two kinds of measurements in printing that are real but not stated in fixed amounts. How's that again? Well, it's something like percentages. A fractional amount doesn't mean anything unless you know what it is a fraction of.

The em measurements are fractions of point sizes. One em is the same width as the type size, whether the size is 6-point, 24-point or whatever. It comes from the fact that the letter *M* is usually as wide as it is high.

There is much misuse of the term "em" in markup under the mistaken notion that an em is a pica. It is only a pica when 12-point type is in use. Printers' proofreaders must be alert to diagnose what is meant when ems are specified. A job marked to be set 18 ems wide is almost certain to be intended to be 18 picas wide. On the other hand, paragraph indention, which should be specified in real ems, can be accepted as such. If indention is specified in picas the reader should be suspicious. To actually set a two-pica indention in 10-point type it would be necessary to set two em-quads plus two, two-point spaces each time.

A linotype font contains ems and ens. An en is one-half of

an em. Below the en, actual point sizes of spacing material are used. For hand setting there are spaces of one-fifth, one-fourth, one-third, one-half and one em. Other spaces are in actual point sizes.

Fractions of ems are used here but in printing jargon a piece of spacing material one-fourth of an em wide is called a "four-to-em" space, meaning four of them equal one em. The other fractional ems are named likewise.

In addition to the confusion of ems with picas there has come to be an attempt to use decimal percentages of picas and to write combinations of picas and points as decimal figures. Faced with a decimal amount the proofreader must make a guess. Either 10.5 or 10.6 picas can be interpreted as 10½ picas—properly written 10 + 6. A measure given as 20.8 usually means 20 picas + 8 points. In photosetting the computer command will usually be, and the printout will show 20p8.

The unit system is also one of relative measurements and is only an extension of the em measurements but even the practical printers have all kinds of misunderstandings of it.

The width of individual type characters was originally random. The hand compositor and linotype operator could control line length with spacing adjustments. When it became necessary for a machine to calculate word space it was necessary to measure everything that occupied space in a line. Type faces were designed or redesigned so that each character would have a definite width. That width is stated in units, which are fractions of ems. How the different kinds of machines handle this is reported in the next chapter but remember there is none of the metallic control of line length in photosetting. A line is as long as the sum of the units going into it.

Once one gets over the hurdle of thinking of a unit as a fraction of an em (the type size), the next step is to adjust to the fact that different typesetting machines measure units differently.

Most of the Photons in use at the moment operate with units of $\frac{1}{18}$ em. At last report the Fototronic and Alphatype were providing $\frac{1}{36}$ em units. The IBM Selectric® Composer uses nine units.

The theory is all that it is necessary to understand. The computers will take care of the arithmetic and measuring. The purpose of lowering the width of units is to achieve finer spacing tolerances. The $\frac{1}{18}$ em unit is a fairly coarse measurement. When the size of the unit is reduced it is possible to adjust the space between letters and the word spaces by minute amounts to suit discriminating typographers.

In practical use a reader may find copy instructions to use 4-unit word spacing on some text matter. In order to know what that comes to in points he must know what kind of units his machine is using. If they are $\frac{1}{36}$ em the 4 units can be figured to be $\frac{4}{36}$ or $\frac{1}{9}$ of an em. For 8-point type the four units would be about 1 point. For 12-point type they would be $1\frac{1}{3}$ points.

General purpose keyboards for photosetting have keys for 8-unit and 4-unit spaces, roughly corresponding to the en and thin-space keys of the linotype.

The weakest point about phototypesetting is the effect created by enlarging negatives to fixed type sizes. On the basic grid of the font the letters will be so proportioned and the spaces between them so allotted as to give as good an effect as can be obtained with metal type. In the metal faces each size is designed so that the letters relate properly. When the lens of the phototypesetter is pulled back to step up to larger sizes it also increases the space around the letters. To combat this it is possible to order the machines to work with fewer units per letter overall or to insert instructions for subtractions of units after particular letters.

It is the judicious use of unit subtractions that divides photosetting between skilled and unskilled work. If the principle is understood the proofreader can judge what can be done or should have been done to improve a job. The unit count of the machines in use and their versatility must be discovered for there are too many models in use and in development to say here what any of them will do.

Once a camera has entered the typesetting picture, type sizes are only approximations and the faces themselves may be distorted by adding prisms.

A reader may be called upon to check that camera instructions have been carried out properly. He is very apt to need to check work that is going to the camera. Most camera work is straight enlarging or reducing and should be expressed in percentages. Graphic arts cameras are calibrated so that a wanted percentage is found on a chart that tells where the copyboard and the lens are to be set and what exposure to use.

It is a remarkable fact that few adults remember how to solve a percentage. Cameramen usually use a calculating wheel that shows the percentage when an original size is lined up with a wanted size. To make the calculation by arithmetic, simply divide the wanted size by the original size. The result is the same whether inches, picas or any other measurement is used. To enlarge from 20 picas to 40 picas divide 40 by 20. The answer is 2.00 or 200%. To make it more difficult, 20 picas enlarged to 25 picas is 25 divided by 20 or 1.25 (125%). Reductions are figured by dividing the smaller number by the larger one—25 picas reduced to 20 picas is 20 divided by 25. The answer is .80 or 80%.

Since an overall percentage reduction changes height in proportion to width, a reader may have need to know what will happen to the height of the type block when the width is changed.

This is best solved graphically. A diagonal line drawn from the corners of a box shows the relative dimensions of height and width at any point along the line. If a box is drawn around a block of type a diagonal line to the point where the desired width is reached will show what the new height will be. A reader finding a job will not reach the desired height when enlarged to the correct width can figure the amount of leading that should be added.

Newspaper measures contain a number of complications. The widths are expressed mainly by number of columns and column widths vary. They change not only from one newspaper to another but from one page or section to another. The *Wall Street Journal* column is 16 picas wide. Some are 10, 10½, 11 and so forth, including bastard measures. Advertisers use SRDS reports to find out the width and cost of a specific newspaper's column. There are other reports for magazines.

There are two widths to take into account in measuring column widths. The columns of type must be separated, so a column is not just a fraction of the page width. A two-column cut or ad is not twice the width of the type used for one column. It is twice the width plus the gutter between the columns. The gutter varies. In hot metal it is apt to be six points, being formed by a six-point rule with a centered hairline. More tolerance is allowed for pasteup of phototype—usually a pica.

Another calculation peculiar to newspapers is shrinkage. In the process of making a mold of the flat type page from which to cast a curved plate for the presses, stereotyping, there is a loss in size of about $2\frac{1}{2}\%$. This does not affect the ordinary typesetting standards. It is only taken into account in large ads. In order to make sure that an advertiser gets his 200 lines when he orders a full tabloid page the original page is made up 205 lines deep.

Although there is no apparent shrinkage necessary in offset presswork the cross-use of ads prepared for hot metal and the fact that the photosetters may produce only six-point type rather than agate make it necessary to shoot completed pages to reduced sizes. The Copley press uses a ratio of $6\frac{1}{2}$ picas to the inch rather than six for its original makeup. There are so many variations that ads prepared for nationwide use are allotted plenty of white space and the preferred corners indicated by small bullets for positioning.

# 14

# Typesetting Methods

BEFORE GOING INTO the many ways that type characters can be arranged for printing it is well to give a brief review of the presses that will pour out the finished printing. The two major kinds of printing are called offset and letterpress.

Letterpress printing is done by running an inked roller over raised surfaces and then contacting the paper with the inked surfaces. A type form for letterpress can be a combination of kinds of printing surfaces containing type, linotype slugs, electroplates, etched plates, plus metal rules or anything else that has a printable surface and is the same height as the rest.

Photographic and metal typesetting are interchangeable at any point along the way. Anything that is to be printed by letterpress can be turned into a metal plate by having it photographed and etched into metal. A proof of metal type can be used for offset.

Offset printing is done from a plate which is perfectly smooth but has the property of rejecting ink everywhere except where photographic images of whatever is to be printed have been exposed onto it by light and a developing process. The plate is a positive image of the type. It is inked, printed onto a rubber roller and the paper is printed from the roller.

In order to make an offset plate there must be a photographic negative or group of negatives mounted together and masked. That is called "stripping." The typesetting phase ends with supplying images to the camera for the negatives. Usually finished artwork, called a "mechanical," is supplied. It can be composed of a combination of typsetting results, just as a metal typeform can—clear proofs of metal type, photographic prints from phototypesetting machines, drawn or pasted rules, or screened photos. There is some misunderstanding of that last item among printing buyers. Just as the letterpress photoengraving must be composed of very small raised dots that can be inked, so must an offset plate have them.

Making a negative and an offset plate from it from positive camera-ready copy is now such a simple process that offset printing in small quantities is very inexpensive. There are machines for going directly from art to print.

A screened print is a little more complicated and though proofreaders don't really have to know how it is done, the principles are not difficult to understand. The curious are sometimes mystified by art accompanying proofs.

To make a screened negative, an ordinary black and white photograph is put on the camera easel in front of the lens and the cameraman focuses to the finished size desired. He then puts a negative in the camera. It's held in position by vacuum suction. A screen goes on top of the negative. There is a choice of screens that will produce different sizes of dots and they are graded by numbers of dots per inch, called line numbers. The usual gradations are 65, 85, 100, 110 and 120 lines. The lowest number is the coarsest screen, used for printing on newsprint.

The cameraman makes an exposure—figuring out the exposure is the only difficult part of the process. What happens during the exposure is that the whitest areas of the photo are nearly burned into solid blacks on the negative. The screen isn't entirely solid. Its opaque areas are graduated enough to let most of the high whites be exposed. Look at any printed photo and you will see very small black dots in the whitest areas, growing larger as the photograph grays down. At the other extreme the blackest areas will not be exposed on the negative, screen or no screen. Since the finished plate of a photo should have some white dots even in the blackest areas an overall exposure is given briefly directly on the screen. There are automatic screen cameras that adjust the screen inside the camera, make the second exposure, chop the film and feed it into a developer.

Sometimes a combination screen and line plate is wanted. This often happens in newspaper advertising containing line and wash drawings and can be obtained by hinging a piece of clear acetate over the drawing. Any lines or solid areas that are to remain that way are covered with black ink on the acetate and the cameraman puts a white sheet of paper between the acetate and drawing for his second exposure. Only the screened areas get the second exposure. The solid blacks remain solid.

A screened negative can be used for any process. It can be used to expose a metal plate for acid etching into a metal engraving. It can be used to directly expose an offset plate for printing or it can be exposed on contact printing paper to be assembled along with type into a finished piece of art that can be photographed by the simple line method.

Proofreaders handling any form of proofs involving halftones (screened cuts) and especially press sheets should take note of the difference in screens. Advertising that is to appear in both newspapers and magazines is made up with the same illustration in both fine and coarse screens. They sometimes get made up with the wrong cut. The dots on a 65-line are easily spotted by the naked eye. A very fine screen requires a magnifier.

*Hand Setting.*

The human hand was the only machine for setting type for some hundreds of years and still is used a lot. For certain typesetting jobs handsetting is not only practical but the most efficient means of producing typesetting.

The advantages of hand setting include the wide variety of typefaces and sizes that can be instantly available, rapidly set and easily corrected. The disadvantages include bad letters caused by wear and damage, and an occasional shortage of type for large jobs or jobs that are held for release by customers. The type must be also redistributed into its case.

Hand-set typography has been considered to be superior to machine typesetting because a skilled compositor can make spacing adjustments to achieve an optimum appearance. A good proofreader can study the proofs and order space in or out for the best appearance.

Prior to the introduction of the photo devices quality typography was judged on the uniformity of apparent space between letters. This was described as "color." Certain letter combinations appear to have more or less space between them than the norm. This can be adjusted to a degree by undercutting such letters as the T and A when they appear together or by adding space between letters with vertical sides that appear too close together.

However, the photosetting machines required that a new approach to what is recognized as good typesetting be promulgated.

The elementary photo printing devices using an alphabet negative for individual exposure of letters left an element of judgment in positioning each letter in relationship to the previous one. Any attempt at hand lettering by an amateur shows how that will wind up.

It was thereupon agreed upon by typographers that good typesetting is that in which all letters be as close to each other as it is possible to get them without overlapping.

It is impossible to live up to that standard in setting type by hand. Type can be shaved on the sides or undercut, and the expensive advertising shops do so, but it is not economically feasible for general work. Tighter word spacing than was formerly the fashion is recommended and is easier to achieve. Note that linotype widows, having been quadded left, use minimum word space.

The compositor's principal tool is the "stick." This is a shallow tray with two solid sides and an adjustable third side that can be set to whatever line length is wanted in aggregates of picas or half-picas. After setting the stick for the type measure desired the compositor cuts a piece of spacing material to that measure, inserts it in the stick and proceeds to the case of type ordered. Once the case has been memorized, setting a line of type is easy. The stick is held in the left hand and as the letters are placed in position the left thumb holds them in position. Word spaces are added to fill the line when the compositor judges an optimum line length has been reached.

### The Ludlow.

The simplest machine for setting metal type is the Ludlow. It sets a single line of type by molding from assembled individual molds of the characters. A stick is used in which the compositor sets the brass molds, just as he would with type, and then tightens a clamp. The stick goes into the molding machine. The comp presses a lever and the line is molded and drops out. The characters in the stick are returned to the case and can be used again for the next line.

A Ludlow line is different from a linotype line in that the letters correspond to the type size on top but are shallow and centered on a pica-wide base. If, for instance, 36-pt type is used the comp puts one pica of spacing material under the letters at the top and bottom.

There are several kinds of stick available. They are graduated in pica markings and a line can be set centered on a measure, justified to a measure or just allowed to come to the necessary length. There are spaces in the same range of widths as for setting hand type. Tightening of letters must be done by setting extra space between the letters to allow for sawing them apart and then trimming the base shorter. The reader can order this to be done.

### The Linotype.

This term is used generically throughout, for most Linotypes and Intertypes perform the same. There are many different kinds of models of both which do special tricks but proofreaders have no need to study them.

Office readers are usually unfamiliar with the possibilities of obtaining good typesetting by linotype and accept bad practices as inevitable.

A linotype is a grotesque machine that looks like some prehistoric monster and they say is doomed to the same extinction. It has served through the lifetimes of some very old printers. It is basically easy to operate—the trick is speed in keyboarding—but operators must also have some facility with mechanical adjustments and in most shops a full-time mechanic is always on duty.

At the top of the machine is a magazine containing the mats (matrices) of one entire type font. Most machines will take several magazines that can be cranked into position to change the font. Each mat has its own channel and drops by gravity into the assembly line when a keyboard key is touched.

Space bands for word spaces are hung above the assembly line separately. They are long, tapered wedges that hang suspended between words and, in casting the line, they are pressed down evenly to spread the words apart enough to fill the line. The keyboard also contains fixed spaces of one em, one en and two points. Smaller spaces of ¼ point, ½ point and 1 point widths can be kept on the side and placed in the line by hand—this is only done in quality shops.

The assembly line is adjustable to given pica widths. As the mats drop into the line a counter moves along and, when it reaches an area where justification is possible, the operator presses a handle that moves the line of mats and space bands into the molding chamber. The machine then automatically makes a mold of the line. An arm lifts the mats and carries them back to the top of the magazine where they drop back into their proper channels according to notches that trigger the correct release point.

There are also type characters, called "sorts," that must be kept on the side and put into the line by hand. These include fractions, Greek letters, accented letters, type refinements like the

Te, To, We, Wo, etc. There are keyboard positions for the ligatures fi, ff, fl, ffi and ffl.

Each mat contains two characters. The second one is the italic or the bold face of the font. In order to cast the second letter there is a rail running along the assembly line on which the mat is hung to raise it so the second character is in the position the first one normally occupies.

Quality linotype work depends on use of proper space bands, the spacing material and sorts. Newspapers have short lines and no time for finesse so they use space bands with maximum width at the top and minimum at the bottom giving ample range of justification. They also use 2-pt minimum thin spaces and if a line doesn't justify easily the operator will letter-space words or syllables with two points between letters.

At the other extreme, spacebands are chosen with a narrow range of taper so that there will be maximum uniformity of word spacing throughout the job. The operator will keep a complete range of spaces alongside the machine and put them into the line by hand at the places that will give the line the best appearance.

Proofreaders must enforce this in accordance with the quality of the work the shop wants to put out. Letter-spacing is sometimes necessary and preferable to excessive word space but it should be uniform throughout the line—never in a single word.

Wrong fonts are a plague of linotype work. When a line of type is set using two different fonts, the operator must halt the machine after casting the line and pull out the mats from the face that is not of the font in use. The machine cannot identify fonts. If a line has started with a word or two of Helvetica and then continued in Times Roman and the mats are allowed to return to the top for redistribution, they will all drop into whichever magazine is in place. They will eventually wind up being reset. This will continue repeating until the wrong font is discovered and removed. The number of mats of a particular character vary according to frequency of its use in the language. A wrong font *s, t,* or *e* is apt to turn up every other line. The reoccurrence forms a uniform pattern and if it shows a break in the pattern a closer check should be made.

It is possible to mix either different faces or different sizes. Sometimes the difference is hard to spot.

Some wrong fonts are so subtly different that the best of readers will miss them some of the time. A careful shop, running any sizable job, will insist that the operator run out the entire font before beginning the job and have a proof of it okayed by a reader. This is easy to do. The keyboard operates like a machine-gun—as long as a key is depressed the mats will continue to fall. The operator just runs down the keyboard holding each key until the channel is empty. A wrong font is easiest to catch when it appears next to the same letter. You may miss a wrong font *l* consistently but if it turns up in *will* you are apt to notice.

The second line of defense against perpetuating wrong fonts is the way the letters and lines on the sides of the mats facing the operator are arranged or colored. An operator can usually spot a wrong font from this if he checks regularly. An isolated wrong font, or a few of them appearing and then disappearing, means that the operator has found it himself but if they are continuing and there is any likelihood that there are still wrong font mats in a magazine, the operator or foreman should be notified immediately. It is best to make a scratch pad note, such as, "WF e, h, t in 10-pt Caledonia." If the font isn't actually being used the note can be attached to the magazine for checking before it is used again. If there are other readers in the proofroom they can be warned of a wrong font that is easy to miss and you can get a brag in at the same time by affecting annoyance.

*The Monotype.*

Monotype isn't as popular as linotype but has some advantages. It consists of two operations, a keyboard that punches a tape and a casting room that uses the tape to cast individual characters and spaces. The keyboard figures the length of lines and widths of spaces necessary to justify the line. The molding machine uses a square grid containing the molds and the tape causes the grid to move up or down, or side to side, to position the correct character in line with the mold.

An advantage in the use of the Monotype is that entire fonts of type can be manufactured in the plant and melted down after one use, providing fresh type for all jobs.

Corrections can be made by hand for simple transpositions or substitutions of letters. There is always the danger of errors being made inside lines between readings.

*Strike-on Machines.*

Offset printing, having eliminated the need for anything more than a photographable image, brought on some devices resembling the typewriter—using the carbon ribbon but adding regular type faces and even justification of words. The *Varityper* has been in use for many years and the *IBM Selectric Composer* has reached the point of an extensive set of faces and sizes. The latest provides justification. Each type font comes complete on one of the "golf balls" which can be dropped into place and snapped on. Fonts are available from 3 to 12 point and the characters designed in a range of nine units which are calculated by the machine as the copy is typed. The space bar can be set in units up to one em. The paper can be advanced in increments of one point. A special ribbon and paper is used for crisp impressions.

*Photosetting.*

The most elementary form of typesetting can be done by anyone. Almost any art supply store will sell you a sheet of alphabets that can be rubbed off onto a white surface. They come in a broad selection of typefaces under the ordinary names of the faces.

Actual phototypesetting from a negative of an alphabet can be done with several simple machines. One of the first was mostly a piece of drafting equipment that allowed the negative to be positioned under a handheld exposure light that moved along a guide that measured the position for the succeeding letter.

*The Filmotype* uses a roll of negative alphabets over a roll of printing paper. A letter is positioned by guidelines and contact exposed. The film and paper, gripped together, are cranked to the end of the guideline for the width of the letter. Then the film is freed from the paper and the next letter cranked into position. When a word or line has been exposed the paper is removed and developed by hand. There are different guidelines that can be selected to close up certain letter combinations but the work is not seen until it is developed.

*The Typositor* is a projection device which can be set for percentages of the size of the film alphabet. It will hold a roll of several fonts of film negatives that can be rapidly cranked into position under the light source, and viewed by safelight. The Typositor has a built-in developing system at the exposure point. The operator cranks a letter into a position under the light source. An exposure is made and by the time the next letter is cranked into position the letter that has been exposed has developed enough to be visible. The paper is advanced by a lever and the operator can position the exposed letter in relation to the next letter to be exposed exactly as he wishes. The paper advances into a stop bath and eventually out of the machine where it is torn off and fixed and washed by hand.

A good operator who keeps the machine clean and the chemicals supplied properly can produce sharp, well-spaced type lines. Calculating the degree of enlargement to fit type into a given layout area is the only difficult part of use of the Typositor. There are auxiliary lenses that will condense or expand the standard type fonts. The fonts are obtainable in a wide range which may be specified by numbers from a specimen book or by their usual standard names. There are also fonts of special faces and sorts—including some of the decorations used in pasteup, such as rounded corners for boxes.

There are several other brands of machines for producing display lines.

Both the linotype and monotype have been adapted to produce photos of type instead of metal. *The Fotosetter* was the first to get into production. The type is set on a linotype keyboard with a photo unit replacing the metal-casting unit. It uses one size of negatives and a turret of 14 lenses, each lens providing a different type size. The Fotosetter justifies by adding letter space while the word spaces remain fixed. The amount of letterspacing is usually small enough to be unobjectionable.

*The Monophoto* uses the monotype keyboard and tape with its grid fonts and casting machinery converted to photo printing. It is comparatively slow in printing but does beautiful work—especially on mathematical formulas. It can store a complicated array of characters such as Greek, foreign letter accents and math symbols. These have to be planned for in advance.

A Monophoto operation in San Jose, where it is used mostly for textbook printing, sets each type size separately on film and strips in the examples and footnotes after editing and proofreading.

*Keyboards.*

The link between metal and phototypesetting machines began with the teletypesetter, although telegraphic transmission of punched tape was in use decades ago. From its offices in Radio City, *Time* punched out the tapes for its Chicago plant.

The Elektron Linotype was developed to make it possible for punched tape, with arrangements of holes corresponding to the keys and commands of the linotype, to operate the machine. The advantages were many. There was no waiting by the machine for an operator to finish a line, no waiting by the operator for the machine to perform its casting operation, and stories punched at one point could be telegraphed anywhere.

The original teletypesetter contained the equivalent keys of the linotype keyboards. It was limited to standard news column widths.

Well, that got complicated with developments of the photo machines and had to be expanded to keyboards of up to 150 keys and computers as intermediaries. There are now several general-purpose keyboards for producing tape that computers can re-punch for the different photosetting machines, although each system comes with its own keyboard and computing system.

*Photosetting Machines.*

There are many brands of photosetting machines on the market, with continuing changes. The ones in widest use include the Photon, Linofilm, Fototronic and Alphatype. Each has different variations but some of the basic principles are similar. There is some litigation over the similarities.

Basically, a square grid or a revolving disk contains the type characters. This is exposed by a Xenon tube, a strobe of such speed as to expose a single character even though it is whirling past the light source. The exposure is beamed through a lens from a turret of lenses, each providing a magnification or reduction to a specific point size. The exposure is captured in a "bird cage," a prismatic device that adjusts to keep odd sizes on the same baseline. From the bird cage the exposure goes to an angled mirror that directs the character to the photographic negative or paper and then moves along a track, the width of the character, to the next character. The photographic paper remains stationary for the length of the line and then moves up the number of points of the type size or whatever advance is ordered in the keyboarding. It usually is fed into an automatic processor and out of the machine.

A line of type is planned in advance by computer calculations. If it is a justified line, the total number of all of the characters in the line are counted and the remaining number of units, allotted to word space, are divided and each word space given a number of units of movement by the mirror.

If the orders include letter-spacing to justify to a full line it will proceed to do that—an annoying trick when a display line that is too long and must be assembled manually comes up.

The photosetting machines, given the proper instructions, are dependable most of the time—but they do have some quirks.

Leading is usually inserted above a line, rather than below it as is done with metal type, which can result in some reversing from what was intended—a subhead jammed against the preceding paragraph and extra space between it and the following paragraph. A block of 8-point type following a 36-point line may overlap the display line.

Wrong fonts are rare but do occur, particularly with the Photon which uses several fonts to a single disk.

An occasional phenomenon is a miscalculation that sends a line slightly beyond the measure. Since newspaper makeup men stick a piece of photo type on a trimmer and slice off the margins as close as they can come to the type, this can cause elimination of the end of a line.

On occasions, machine trouble will result in crowding of some letters and letter-spacing of others.

Bad commands can result in entire jobs being set in the wrong face or measure and this can usually be remedied best by returning the job to the keyboarding department where correct commands are punched and attached to the beginning of the tape.

Although direct keyboarding on the photosetting machine keyboards allows for typographic niceties like back spacing by the unit, most computer setting leaves undesirable spacing gaps which are better referred to the pasteup department for correction by knife.

*Cathode ray* typesetting gets into such advanced electronics that the mechanics are beyond lay comprehension. The typesetting is done at a fairly simplified keyboard with what looks like a small television screen behind it. The operator can see the result of the work on the screen and correct lines with errors. The keyboarding is transmitted to a tape that will replay it for the proofroom's screen for proper proofreading and the reader can make his corrections by keyboard. The corrected tape is then processed by a computer and printed by the cathode ray tube. This device actually draws the characters by horizontal and vertical sweeps of light beams.

Again, the first hard-copy print (the "type") must go to editing and proofreading. Corrections are merged into the computer's magnetic tape and it will then proceed to formulate page makeup and process a complete set of pages or an entire book.

*Optical Recognition Devices.*

The optical recognition devices are capable of reading from typed manuscripts and transferring the copy into typesetting instructions. They require a special form of typewriter face recognizable to the scanner. IBM has a readable "golf ball." They will accept corrections, either on the manuscript they are scanning or insert corrections separately, from correction or insertion copy.

There are several forms of these devices. One uses a combined form of key in which the regular typing is underscored with code marks consisting of varying width vertical lines and these lines are what the machine recognizes. The editor or proofreader can read from the normal typewriter type.

There are a variety of devices for correcting manuscripts to be fed into scanning setters. One is a symbol that deletes a wrong letter, used twice it deletes the preceding word and used three times it deletes the entire line. There is an insert code that can be used to indicate matter to be inserted. One system for editing and proofreading is to draw a black horizontal line through a word that is to be changed and make the correction in red or blue ink. The scanner cannot see red or blue but the black line stops its operation and it searches below the line for the correction. The typist correcting the manuscript types in the correction in the space below the line with the correction, using // or deltas for a deletion or the correct wording preceded and ended by codes.

As in reading other printouts involving coded instructions to the computer, reading from a cathode ray tube or copy for an optical scanning device includes understanding of the instruction codes. Probably no two are exactly the same.

# 15

# Computers

COMPUTERS AREN'T quite as bad as most people believe them to be. They may be stupid, stubborn and expensive beyond practical value in many cases but they do perform amazing feats. The expense factor may be overridden in the short run for large operations by reduction of work force. Maybe the economists should ask one whether it is practical to replace skilled labor with government subsistence.

In typesetting, a computer can take instructions from a keyboard through the medium of punched tape or directly onto its magnetic tapes or cores and do several tricks with it. Through its memory tapes it can translate or store what it has received and reissue new tapes or instructions to the photosetting machines.

With all of the many forms of keyboarding and the vast array of typesetting machinery requiring individual forms of address, the computer serves as an intermediary as well as a high-speed calculating machine.

One elementary example is wire tape. The news services can send out their stories, combining copy and punched tape to all of their newspapers, ready to feed into the linotypes. But to a newspaper using a different measure or a photosetter it is necessary that

the tape received be repunched to operate under the new requirements. The reverse is also used. A scanner can punch tape for
linotypes.

The computer's most popular trick is the one of justifying
lines. Humans do a better job of it but a somewhat slower one. No
practical way of teaching a computer to divide words has yet been
developed. The lines of attack are to eliminate divisions entirely
and in line with that is the popularity of ragged typesetting. The
other approach is called logic. The computer can be told that it is
logical to divide between two letter *t*'s. It cannot understand that
there is a difference between *put-ting* and *putt-ing*. Nor can it
realize that *Pit-tsburgh* is improper. The next step is to feed it an
extensive memory of word exceptions.

At the best, any reader will find divisions that need changing.
Popular newspaper practice is to overlook bad divisions. If it is
necessary to change one, the computer can be overridden by the
operator by finding a correct break that will provide a shorter
line and insert a hyphen followed by a JUSTIFY command. In patch
corrections, as used on newspapers, the remainder of the paragraph
must be punched. It should also be when there is any possibility
that a correction line will not be the same length as a line containing an error. In programs with merge instructions, the computer may refigure the entire remainder of the job following a correction that disrupts its plans.

The computer trick that is hardest on the readers is the
printout. Examples of that have already been given in the chapter
on marks. Printouts can be treacherous to work with and difficult
to learn but there are advantages. Wire service copy, for instance,
simplifies the reader's job by making it unnecessary to follow
copy. Presumably, what appears on the type is the same as what
is on the copy. Editorial corrections have to be carried but the
remainder of the reading is just scanning. Mostly, wire tape is used
for the interminable reports of sports events and box scores.

Stock market reports come direct from the computers at the
exchanges and require no reading from copy.

The treacherous part of printout reading is catching all of the coded instructions. An elementary trap is an order to switch to italics. If the command to return to roman is omitted the entire remainder of the job will continue in italics. There are unlimited possibilities for errors of this sort.

Some programs have safeguards against incorrect commands that will either turn the remaining printout to gibberish or complain that "THIS IS AN ILLEGAL COMMAND" and refuse to proceed.

When a job is fed into a computer it can be given a number and can be stored in the memory tape for as long as necessary. It can be wiped out by setting a new job using the same number just as on a home tape recorder. This is a boon to typesetting plants, where storage of type awaiting corrections or killing is a big problem. For directories and catalogs it is an immense advantage.

Special format codes can be fed to a computer. A common example is one of those food store ads where a listing of pretended bargains may contain a line of 12-point descriptive matter flush left above a line of 24-point telling the kind of food, leadered out to two or three lines of 8-pt. caps telling the size of can and a price set in 36-pt type with the dollar or cent sign set in 18-pt. All of the necessary adjustments in the photo unit are planned by the markup department and expressed in computer codes which are headed by a format number.

The operator can then begin punching the copy with the format number and only has to punch the MERGE key for each change. The entire block of copy will come out of the photo unit, in position, ready for paste-up. An entire ad or an entire book can be plotted in this way, but there is a point where it is faster to assemble chunks of copy by pasteup than to plan all of the movements and risk an error somewhere along the way that will garble the whole job.

Once a format has been fed to the computer it can be used over again indefinitely or cancelled.

Where a format is used regularly it is usually stored. Standardized government publications and newspaper editorial matter find it useful. Advertising departments hold little hope for any practical advantage.

While it is facetious to describe these practical functions of computers as tricks, the real virtue of the computer in typesetting is its enormous speed in calculating the arithmetical control of photosetting machines. In the first Linofilm installation at the *New York Daily News* the operation of the machines was handled by operators with no typing skills. It was necessary for the operator to select a type face and measure and chart out the number of units a line would contain. A unit counter on the keyboard would show the total units available. The operator would then laboriously peck out the words of the copy and after each character the unit counter would subtract the number of units of that character until a decision to justify was reached.

That example is given to show the enormous speed of a computer in making decisions for overall changes and keeping track of the arithmetic of all the changes, and then putting the result through the photo unit in one unhesitating movement.

# 16

# Typefaces

THE PROOFREADERS AT the top of the trade are those with a sound knowledge of typeface identification. It isn't that the knowledge is of vast importance in many kinds of jobs where other abilities are paramount. It is mainly that, in the acquiring of the knack, there is a demonstration of acquired experience at the work under demanding conditions.

This is a self-taught subject. There are books that have attacked the problem. They can be helpful but have the common failing of trying for a logical approach, showing too many faces that are rarely used, and not going into the variations of particular faces.

This chapter will attack the recognition problem—ordinarily a reader's only responsibility—by pointing out the pitfalls in the naming and describing of typefaces and by concentrating on the most commonly used faces.

The first problem a reader encounters is the type specimen book. There can be a problem for even the most experienced reader in learning what faces any particular shop carries. There will be different names for the same faces and in Monotype or photosetting each face will be represented by a number.

Novices should beware of learning from a specialized specimen book, but a general one is hard to find. Even the books of one-line specimens provided by typesetters are guarded carefully. They are expensive to produce. The best buy in a general sample book is *Specimens of Type Faces in the United States Government Printing Office* which could be bought recently for $1.25.

Another step is to find a good book to study, such as *Encyclopedia of Type Faces,* Jaspert, Berry and Johnson, published in the United States under the imprint of Barnes and Noble, in the library.

The naming of typefaces and descriptions of their variations, such as width and boldness, is a wonderland that can defy the most orderly mind. There is just enough consistency in describing these factors to expect a descriptive term to hold true for all faces. It doesn't.

Futura Medium is practically identical to Vogue Bold. Century Expanded is more condensed than Century Schoolbook. Helvetica Bold in the linotype version is about as bold as Helvetica Medium in the foundry type.

Most faces come in varying degrees of boldness. Some of the descriptive names are: extra light, light, book, medium, demibold, semibold, heavy, bold, extrabold, black and ultrabold.

There are also versions that are of different width. Some of the width variations are called: extra condensed, condensed, elongated, narrow, compressed, expanded, extended and wide.

Within these comparatives there is usually a middle point where only the name of the face is used and there is a temptation to use the word "regular." Since a face may be regular or normal in several ways the description in a type specification is ambiguous. It may refer to width, boldness, or roman as opposed to italic. In specifications, the regular width and normal weight are supplied if only the name of the face is mentioned.

It is sometimes helpful or necessary to set up groups of typefaces having some common similarity, in order to discuss the group or arrange them in type specimen books for the convenience of typographers in selecting typefaces. There is no standard practice for naming such groups. The two principal separations are faces with and without serifs. The ones with serifs may be called old style, reader, book, or text. The ones without are sans serif or gothic. Specimen books may also separate faces by means of setting: as lino, hand, ludlow, typositor, or a particular photo-setting machine.

There are two routes for identification of typefaces and the first is the same one we use in recognizing people's faces—an instant overall recognition. Everyone who reads is familiar with the most commonly used faces, but most have never been introduced and don't know the names.

The other route is checking of certain characteristics. Some of these are the broad ones by which faces are separated into groups, like those with serifs and those without. Then there are tighter groups within the main groupings where there are general similarities of shapes of letters—round, oval or square. Finally there are the distinctive touches of the individual letters.

When it comes to distinctive characteristics, you will find very few that can be assigned to one specific face. Garamond has a unique straight line in the connecting line of the g and one vertical serif opposed to a slanted serif in the T. The open g in Baskerville is unusual but is duplicated in Cheltenham. And so it goes, with more and more duplications to eliminate till you arrive at the combination of characteristics that proves identity of the face.

There aren't too many things that can be done to a letter and still keep it recognizable. In hand lettering the beginner is taught to make just four strokes: vertical, horizontal, and the left and right curves. Everything else is decoration. Using the basic strokes, with a chisel-pointed pencil or pen, several variations can be achieved. The width of the point, when held steady in drawing the curves, will determine the amount of variation in thickness of the curved lines. Typefaces having such variation follow this pat-tern.

The cross-strokes of the T, t, E, e, F, f, H and A can be high, low or centered, as can the height of the loop on the R and P.

There is another proportion that is important in identification for which there is no common name. It is sometimes referred to as "lettersize" and is the height of the letters m, n, w, r, s, z, x, c, v and the vowels a, e, o and u. To avoid misunderstanding, this dimension will be referred to as the *vowel* height. An ascender, of course, is the portion of the letter rising above this vowel height and a descender extends below.

(Make note that most old-style faces have alternate short and long descenders. This book is set with short descenders.)

The cap height is the height of the capitals, which are usually the same height as each other and the full height of the b, d and l.

This relationship between the vowel height and cap height will be used frequently in describing the characteristics of the typefaces. In the following rundown of the principal faces the descriptions are of the regular versions of the faces, unless something unusual about the variations is noted.

Phototypesetting machines use the same faces as the metal ones but there are variations to provide for standard widths in units. Some systems adopt a new name for a face. Usually they pick a related name. Scotch Roman is an old face rarely used. It was redesigned to become the very popular Caledonia. The Intertype Corporation renamed their Fototronic version Laurel.

*Sans Serif Faces.*

The first group of faces discussed here consists of those faces of uniform thickness and no serif.

*Futura* is the best known of these. It is the most easily identified of faces because it is drafted entirely with straight lines and circles. The O is a perfect circle and the C a chopped-off circle. The R has a section of a circle butted against the vertical stroke and so forth.

ABCDEFGHIJKLMNOPQRSTUVWXYZ
abcdefghijklmnopqrstuvwxyz          &$1234567890

*Spartan* and *Vogue* are substituted freely for *Futura*. They are machine versions with a few minor variations.

In the *Futura* series the vowels are unusually small, only about half the cap height. Thus *Futura* letters have the appearance of being a size smaller than the same size of other typefaces.

Other faces are occasionally used that bear strong resemblance to *Futura*. Some are *Metro, Tempo, Spartan, Techno,* and *Airport Black*.

Outside the *Futura* family, the principal sans-serif, equal-line faces in present use are *News Gothic, Helvetica, Standard, Folio, Venus* and *Univers*. They all come in a wide range of weights and widths and have enough similarity to make identification difficult.

*News Gothic* has the most classic proportions. You can put the characteristics of other faces of the same general appearance against those of *News* and describe them better than you can *News*. The middle cross strokes are centered, the curved letters are curved evenly and gracefully. The hook on the r has less hook and rises more steeply than in the other faces. Normally *News* has a closed g but it comes with an open one also for those who prefer it that way.

ABCDEFGHIJKLMNOPQRSTUVWXYZ
ABCDEFGHIJKLMNOPQRSTUVWXYZ
abcdefghijklmnopqrstuvwxyz    &$1234567890

**ABCDEFGHIJKLMNOPQRSTUVWXYZ**
**ABCDEFGHIJKLMNOPQRSTUVWXYZ**
**abcdefghijklmnopqrstuvwxyz    &$1234567890**

There are other names for *News Gothic*. Record Gothic is the ludlow version of News Gothic Bold. There is a machine face called *Trade Gothic* that is nearly identical. There is a noticeable difference only in the boldface.

ABCDEFGHIJKLMNOPQRSTUVWXYZ
abcdefghijklmnopqrstuvwxyz    &$1234567890

*News Gothic* is called by its own name in the condensed and extra condensed versions of the regular face but the boldface condensations become known as Alternate Gothic. There are three Alternate Gothics, numbering up from the skinniest which is Alternate Number 1. Number 2 is the most commonly used, coming on the same linotype mat as News Gothic Condensed.

ABCDEFGHIJKLMNOPQRSTUVWXYZ
abcdefghijklmnopqrstuvwxyz                    &$1234567890

**ABCDEFGHIJKLMNOPQRSTUVWXYZ**
**abcdefghijklmnopqrstuvwxyz**                **&$1234567890**

*Helvetica* is *News Gothic*'s closest rival in popularity. It has greater width in relation to height and has shorter ascenders and descenders. The E has a center stroke nearly as long as the top and bottom strokes. The e comes very close to being entirely closed. The top and bottom endings of the S and s are nearly horizontal.

**ABCDEFGHIJKLMNOPQRSTUVWXYZ**
**abcdefghijklmnopqrstuvwxyz          &$1234567890**

*Folio* is cut smaller in proportion to its body sizes than any of the other gothics mentioned here. Part of the top of the body is unused. In some sizes it appears to be a full size smaller. There are only subtle distinctions otherwise and about the only letter that can't be found to have its counterpart in one or more of the other faces is the *a* which has a brief change in direction where the top of the curve joins the vertical stroke. *Folio* has two kinds of R's. The line that changes the P to R is straight in one and curved in the other. Very frequently the two are both used in the same line. These should be made uniform with a preference shown on the proof.

**ABCDEFGHIJKLMNOPQRSTUVWXYZ&**
**abcdefghijklmnopqrstuvwxyz $1234567890**

*Venus* is only a shade taller than *Folio* but it has some unique features that make it easily recognizable. The E has the center stroke well above center and the A has the cross stroke well below center. The previously mentioned faces all have flat tops on the t but the *Venus* t has a chisel top.

ABCDEFGHIJKLMNOPQRSTUVWXYZ&
abcdefghijklmnopqrstuvwxyz  $1234567890

*Univers* is most recognizable by the slight extra space at the sides of letters giving it the appearance of being letter-spaced. There are also frequent occurrences of hairlines of space running into the junctures of vertical and diagonal strokes—note the N. The O is squarish. It has the chisel point on the t but shorter above the cross. *Univers* has no names for widths, weights or italics, all of which are indicated by numbers. Italics are the next higher even number. What could be called light regular is No. 45 and its italic is No. 46. Bold extended is No. 83 and there is a full range between that and No. 39—light extra condensed.

**ABCDEFGHIJKLMNOPQRSTUVWXYZ&**
**abcdefghijklmnopqrstuvwxyz $1234567890**

*Standard* is popular in both display types and for text matter. The name for the machine version is *Akzidenz Grotesk*. The machine form is more distinctive than the handset form. It has longer ascenders than the other gothics of this group. The t is unusually long above the cross. The open letters of Standard are generally chopped off in a pie-cut—as though a knife had been placed in the center of the o and used to create the e, c, C and S.

**ABCDEFGHIJKLMNOPQRSTUVWXYZ&**
**abcdefghijklmnopqrstuvwxyz $1234567890**

Although *Akzidenz* is designated *Grotesk,* and *Venus* is referred to by some as one of the faces of the group called grotesque, they are cut on quite conventional lines. There are several gothic faces that have some actual grotesqueries, the most noticeable being the long downsweep of the hook on the r. The following are used fairly frequently but not enough to make memorizing necessary: *Advertising Grotesk, Headline, Aurora,* and *Inserat Grotesk.* They are all condensed and their vowels occupy nearly the full height of the type body, with ascenders and descenders barely indicated.

Grotesque No. 8, 9, and 18 are similar faces, but fuller in width, with grotesque distortion of the rounded lines, but longer ascenders.

The thick and thin sans serif gothics group has two overwhelmingly popular representatives. The classic standby, *Franklin Gothic,* is easy to recognize and is deservedly in wide use. Two weights of stroke are used for straight horizontals, verticals and diagonals, and the curves graduate gracefully from one to the other. It comes only in one weight but in width graduations of extra condensed, condensed, normal and wide. Note that between the I and l there are eight pieces of type in any size that are straight vertical strokes and the eye must be trained to spot a wrong font letter or a substitution. The O is squarer than the cipher but the same problem exists.

**ABCDEFGHIJKLMNOPQRSTUVWXYZ&**
**abcdefghijklmnopqrstuvwxyz $1234567890**

**ABCDEFGHIJKLMNOPQRSTUVWXYZ&**
**abcdefghijklmnopqrstuvwxyz**          **$1234567890**

**ABCDEFGHIJKLMNOPQRSTUVWXYZ&**
**abcdefghijklmnopqrstuvwxyz**          **$1234567890**

*Optima,* a comparative newcomer, uses a greater variance between the thick and thin strokes and swings into more loosely drawn curves while still maintaining a dignified appearance. It comes in two weights, normal and semibold, but only one width. *Optima* may be thought of as a cleaned-up version of *Lydian*. *Lydian* has about the same weight differential but the appearance of having been done with a chisel-point pen or brush in two or more strokes that barely join.

ABCDEFGHIJKLMNOPQRSTUVWXYZ&
abcdefghijklmnopqrstuvwxyz $1234567890
**ABCDEFGHIJKLMNOPQRSTUVWXYZ&**
**abcdefghijklmnopqrstuvwxyz $1234567890**

*Square Serif Faces.*

The square-serif faces are uniform-line gothics with serifs of the same weight. Typewriters have this kind of face and a cleaner form of it than most of the typefaces. There are linotype and hand type faces called *Typewriter* and are usually so specified though there is more than one cutting—Remington, Underwood and Bulletin.

The other square-serif faces in principal use are Memphis, Cairo, Stymie, Beton and Karnak. They are all similar to each other, and mechanically drawn with the circle being used to form curves. Again memorizing the differences is not too important since in most shops only a chosen one is available.

**ABCDEFGHIJKLMNOPQRSTUVWXYZ**
**ABCDEFGHIJKLMNOPQRSTUVWXYZ**
abcdefghijklmnopqrstuvwxyz    &$1234567

*Reader Faces.*

The faces having serifs are varied and many, and description of the most popular ones here may fit others that aren't even mentioned. As a point of reference and for practical study of the ones most used the first group is limited to Times Roman, Garamond, Caslon, Century, Caledonia, Baskerville and Bodoni. The chances are about even that any particular job will be set in one of these if a serif face is used.

The most popular of them all is *Times Roman*. It's a handsome face, although its most distinctive quality, the chiseled points on the serifs, is often lost by using it in reverses and on coarse stock. The capital letters come right out of the Roman stone cutters' art. The lower case maintains the chiseled effect. The t has no real ascender at all—just a thorn growing out of the cross. The boldface isn't so sharp-pointed but being bolder than most reader faces the sharp little serifs maintain its distinctiveness. This book is set in Times Roman.

ABCDEFGHIJKLMNOPQRSTUVWXYZ
ABCDEFGHIJKLMNOPQRSTUVWXYZ
abcdefghijklmnopqrstuvwxyz                              &$1234567890

*Garamond* has pointed serifs too but it has more unusual letters than other faces. The unique T and g have already been mentioned. The vowel size is small in proportion to the cap height and the swinging ascenders and descenders. There is a noticeable difference in the heights of different vowels.

ABCDEFGHIJKLMNOPQRSTUVWXYZ
ABCDEFGHIJKLMNOPQRSTUVWXYZ
abcdefghijklmnopqrstuvwxyz          &$1234567890

*Baskerville* is the last word in dignity and class. It has the chiseled features too but more of the calligrapher's touch than the stone carver's. There are subtle variations in the proportions of vertical strokes but never wandering away from the overall proportions of the letters. It is larger in vowel size than Times Roman or Garamond. The three have a common characteristic in the e which has a small, high closed portion in all. The top of the T is extremely wide in Baskerville and there are widenings to smooth out angles in the E and L.

ABCDEFGHIJKLMNOPQRSTUVWXYZ
ABCDEFGHIJKLMNOPQRSTUVWXYZ 1234567890
abcdefghijklmnopqrstuvwxyz     &$1234567890

*Caslon* is one of the oldest living faces. It isn't difficult to identify Caslon in general but there are so many cuttings of the face that verifying the correct one and weeding out the wrong fonts is a job for an expert. A few of them are Old Face, New Caslon, Caslon Bold, Number 137, Number 540 and so forth. In general, they have a distinctive A with a concave top, a nipple sticking up at each side of the top of the T and a wideswept top on the f although that varies. The C is usually horseshoe shaped.

ABCDEFGHIJKLMNOPQRSTUVWXYZ
ABCDEFGHIJKLMNOPQRSTUVWXYZ
abcdefghijklmnopqrstuvwxyz          &$1234567890

The chances are that when you learned to read the big letters on the cards were *Century.* Remember the a? The serifs square off somewhat in Century, the only real point being on the t. There is a full hook at the base of the R. The vowel size is medium large. The letters are mostly no-nonsense ones, drawn with the sole purpose of being distinctly themselves. There are three forms of Century for text use plus the condensed display face, *Century Nova. Century Schoolbook* is widest and boldest. *Century Expanded* is the mysteriously misnamed condensed version. *Century Old Style* isn't used often. The italics of Schoolbook and Expanded are totally different in serif styles but are often mixed. The Expanded resembles script in the curves of the serifs.

ABCDEFGHIJKLMNOPQRSTUVWXYZ
ABCDEFGHIJKLMNOPQRSTUVWXYZ
abcdefghijklmnopqrstuvwxyz          &$1234567890
*ABCDEFGHIJKLMNOPQRSTUVWXYZ*
*abcdefghijklmnopqrstuvwxyz          &$1234567890*

ABCDEFGHIJKLMNOPQRSTUVWXYZ
ABCDEFGHIJKLMNOPQRSTUVWXYZ
abcdefghijklmnopqrstuvwxyz          &$1234567890
*ABCDEFGHIJKLMNOPQRSTUVWXYZ*
*ABCDEFGHIJKLMNOPQRSTUVWXYZ*
*abcdefghijklmnopqrstuvwxyz          &$1234567890*

*Caledonia,* the modern cutting of *Scotch Roman,* is one of the most popular book faces. It's one of the few old style faces with a flat top on the t. The vowel size is large and the ascenders slightly higher than the capitals.

ABCDEFGHIJKLMNOPQRSTUVWXYZ
ABCDEFGHIJKLMNOPQRSTUVWXYZ
abcdefghijklmnopqrstuvwxyz &$1234567890

*Bodoni* goes way back in history, its designer being a contemporary of William Caslon, but the modern version has been drawn more mechanically. It is mentioned at this point because the text version, *Bodoni Book,* is somewhat similar to the other faces in the group and fairly high in popularity. The straight hairline serifs make it unmistakable but are not so noticeable at the 8-point reader level.

ABCDEFGHIJKLMNOPQRSTUVWXYZ
ABCDEFGHIJKLMNOPQRSTUVWXYZ
abcdefghijklmnopqrstuvwxyz &$1234567890

ABCDEFGHIJKLMNOPQRSTUVWXYZ
ABCDEFGHIJKLMNOPQRSTUVWXYZ
abcdefghijklmnopqrstuvwxyz &$1234567890

*Display Faces.*

Beyond the *Bodoni Book* level there are many forms of the original design—some called by different names but for purposes of learning identification they can be grouped as a family by the generic hairline serifs and cross-strokes. The bolder versions lead into the faces that are used more for heads than text.

The face called simply *Bodoni* corresponds to what is usually described as boldface. It's similar enough to Century Bold in weight and proportion to be substituted in correction lines if the reader isn't paying attention. There is also the danger of confusing it with the real *Bodoni Bold,* a definitely bolder version.

**ABCDEFGHIJKLMNOPQRSTUVWXYZ**
**ABCDEFGHIJKLMNOPQRSTUVWXYZ**
**abcdefghijklmnopqrstuvwxyz    &$1234567890**

*Ultra Bodoni* is the darling of the department stores and everywhere else where a very bold but handsome display line is wanted. It is also called *Poster Bodoni, Engravers Bodoni* and *Modern Bodoni.*

**ABCDEFGHIJKLMNOPQRSTUVWXYZ&**
**abcdefghijklmnopqrstuvwxyz $123456789**

The Bauer foundry in Germany has a slightly different cutting of its Bodoni, particularly a slight curve in the hairlines. The designation is either *Bauer Bodoni* or *German Bodoni* and few shops carry both it and the American version.

*Torino* and *Onyx* are in fairly common use and can be learned by their similarity in hairline serifs to Bodoni although they are considerably different in weight and totally dissimilar to other faces.

What can loosely be called the *Cheltenham* family of faces includes those with serifs approximating the weight of the letters but still serif-shaped—not the equal weight strokes of the square serifs. The bold versions of the old-style faces meet this description too but *Cheltenham, Clarendon, Consort, Egizio* and *Fortune* are primarily designed for display use.

Cheltenham was once the mainstay for newspaper headlines, particularly the extra condensed which could be used 13 cap letters to the line in one-column heads.

ABCDEFGHIJKLMNOPQRSTUVWXYZ&
abcdefghijklmnopqrstuvwxyz $1234567890

*Clarendon* has the qualities of Cheltenham in the capitals but increases the vowel size in proportion to cap height drastically. The *Craw Clarendons,* though differing slightly in design and width, are varied in boldness to fit between the *Haas Clarendons.* In progressive steps of boldness there are: *Craw Book, Clarendon, Craw Clarendon* and *Clarendon Bold. Craw Modern* and *Craw Modern Bold* look more like Bodoni in that they have some near hairlines but the serifs are by no means pure line. *Consort* is similar to Clarendon. It has even more width to the serifs with consequent narrowing of the width of the letter forms, a quality that makes good spacing of the letters very difficult.

ABCDEFGHIJKLMNOPQRSTUVWXYZ&
abcdefghijklmnopqrstuvwxyz $1234567890

**ABCDEFGHIJKLMNOPQRSTUVWXYZ&
abcdefghijklmnopqrstuvwxyz $12345670**

*Fortune* can be considered as the most extended version of Clarendon.

**ABCDEFGHIJKLMNOPQRSTUVWX&
abcdefghijklmnopqrstuvwxyz $1234567**

Although some of the originals were designed a long time ago, some of the squared-off faces have developed a great deal of popularity only recently. *Melior, Micrograma* and *Eurostile* are ordered so frequently that they should be learned. Basically, *Micrograma* and *Eurostile* are the same. The former comes only in caps but the latter has lower case also. In each case the round letters are squares with rounded corners. Since there is no exact corresponding weight and condensation or expansion there is no problem of getting the two mixed.

ABCDEFGHIJKLMNOPQRSTUVWXYZ&
abcdefghijklmnopqrstuvwxyz $1234578

There are other faces with the squaring approach but if *Melior* is studied well, they can be left to identification from the specimen book. Melior graduates the curves a little gentler than Eurostile and has thicks and thins and serifs. The regular and bold versions are wide, the vowel height large and the descenders very short. There is a high cross-stroke on the A but it is centered on the e, E, F, and H.

ABCDEFGHIJKLMNOPQRSTUVWXYZ&
abcdefghijklmnopqrstuvwxyz    $1234567890

*Copperplate Gothic,* as has been mentioned, comes in numbered sizes within the point sizes and getting the correct size is the only problem. Generally it is numbered upwards but there are printers who reverse that order and also another numbering system. The face is easy to identify because of the minute serifs. They represent the flick of the engraving tool from the time when personal social cards were engraved by hand on copper. *Liteline Gothic* is sometimes used for the same purposes as Copperplate, comes in the numbered sizes, but doesn't have the nick. It resembles the letter forms used by draftsmen for hand lettering.

**ABCDEFGHIJKLMNOPQRSTUVWXYZ**
**1234567890&**

When you go to a general type book you are going to find hundreds of faces not mentioned here. From time to time some of them are requested in typesetting shops. There is a temptation to include more but it would only cause unnecessary distraction. The ones that are omitted have either the quality of being unique enough to pose no problem of identification or are similar cuttings to the widely used faces mentioned.

The best way of learning to recognize a face is to try to copy it by hand. It isn't necessary to do the whole alphabet but enough letters should be tried to note the similarity of lines and curves. This helps not only in identification but in the spotting of wrong fonts. Although there are differences in the drawing of particular letters, the width of strokes and the way the curves are handled are always uniform for each letter of a face. Some letters are only portions of other letters—the F is a part of the E, the P a part of the R. The most distinctive letters are the t, r, a, e, f and g in the lower case and the A, E, G, T and R in the capitals.

The many variations in width and boldness of individual faces have only been touched on for specific faces and getting the right version is important, but the first step is recognizing the basic cutting of the faces. Do it a face at a time, but regularly, and it will save years of forced cramming under pressure.

# 17

# The Jargon

JARGON IS LANGUAGE peculiar to a trade or profession. The common words used in printing and publishing for discussing jobs, or as instructions on copy and proofs, have specialized and overlapping meanings. The journeyman who really journeys is continually finding things referred to in terms he knows by different meanings.

This chapter is organized—or disorganized—to show the overlapping meanings more than to define. Simple definitions are alphabetical but the words that are tied together are taken up in bulk.

*Art.* This is an outstanding example of a word that covers many printing terms. Mainly it separates that part of copy that is to be set in type from any other form of material that is to go into a job. It can mean illustrations, type that is to be picked up, or plates. A *plate,* in turn, can be many things. Specifically, it is a short form for *electroplate* which is a solid reproduction in copper or zinc of a type form. It is made by making a wax impression of the form and electroplating it. But *plate* can be used broadly to cover stereotype plates, plastic-molded plates, engravings and off-set plates. *Stereotype plates* are made by molding from a kind of cardboard mold called a *mat*. They can be made flat for page makeup or as complete pages, curved to fit cylindrical presses. Offset plates are thin and flexible plates that will hold photo images and, when dampened, reject ink otherwise. For short runs they may be treated paper. To *replate* means to make over a page for another edition. An *engraving* is a plate made by sensitizing metal, photographing the material to be printed and etching out the white space with acid. (That's an engraving for general printing. In artists' engravings for etchings the black area is etched to trap the ink.) An engraving can contain type, line drawings, photographs, or any combination. If it is of a photograph it is called a *halftone,* the continuous tone of the original having been broken down to various sized solid dots that can be printed. A halftone isn't necessarily a plate. It can be a screened photograph for offset makeup. *Cut* usually refers to a halftone. A *logotype* or *adcut* is specifically a piece of type with a special device that has been cast by a type foundry in type-high metal. The most common use of logotypes is for company names and trademarks. Because of this it is customary to call any standing company signature, standing head or title a *logo*. Again it extends to a photo of one for offset.

*Basis.* Paper thickness is specified by the weight of 500 sheets, one ream, of standard size for the paper. Standard sizes: Bond, ledger and writing paper, 17 x 22. (Note that when you chop a sheet that size into four pieces the result is $8\frac{1}{2}$ x 11, the standard stationery size and about the only one worth remembering.) Book papers, 25 x 38. Cover papers 20 x 26. Basis is also called substance weight. It is more useful to learn to refer to paper *stock* as *bible, newsprint, coated, card* and *cover*.

*Bearers.* Type-high metal used around the sides of a type form in order to take an even impression. If there is much white space inside the form, bearers are used there too. The bearers are trimmed off reproduction proofs or sawed or routed from plates.

*Bleed.* A printed area exceeding the finished size. Usually a job that is to bleed is printed one-eighth of an inch larger than the finished size and trimmed on a paper cutter to size. The part that is trimmed off and discarded is the bleed. The finished job is said to bleed—using the word as a verb.

*Burn.* To expose with light. The exposure of an offset plate is most frequently called burning, but the term is used on regular camera work most frequently in connection with the term *double burn* which specifically is double exposure. A simple example is a job with certain sections screened. The negative is exposed with a screen over the entire film. The areas where the screen is wanted are covered on the easel, the screen is removed from the film, and a second exposure burns out the unwanted screen.

*Butt* or *bump.* Both mean "join." Linotype slugs are butted against each other end-to-end to make longer lines than the machine will cast. In low quality work they are all cast in equal lengths and not too much attention is paid to getting even spacing. In good work alternate length lines are set so that there will be no apparent *river* down the center of the job. *Bump* refers mostly to closing up words, as MacBird rather than Mac Bird.

*Caption.* Words that go with pictures are sometimes called *cutlines* or *legends.* A caption is literally a headline to a legend.

*Chase.* A chase is a steel frame in which type is *locked* into position. Actually the type is wedged in with metal wedges called *quoins.*

*Color break.* Color printing may be prepared by *process color*—separation into the primary colors on camera using filters

—or by color break in an art department or composing room. In the latter, a separate form is prepared for each color and the proofroom checks each for accuracy and color register.

*Copy.* The dictionary comes closest to printing copy in the definition "that which is to be reproduced." *Manuscript* is used in book work. Identifying copy that is to be set is a basic problem in job work. The main guideline is that it contain typesetting instructions. Layouts accompanying copy often have copy that has been omitted from the typescript. They also frequently contain different wording—in which case the rule is to use the typescript copy. Newspapers are now retyping advertising copy for markup convenience and adding additional errors. If the advertiser's copy is included it takes precedence. *Camera-ready copy* is final art.

*Copy cutter.* On a newspaper, the person who receives copy and routes parts of it, as the body text to linotype and the heads to ludlow. The job now includes feeding tape to the computers.

*Docket.* There are different terms for the containers of the assembled records, proofs, artwork, photos and so forth that accumulate with a particular job. Book shops use *docket.* Trade plants use *ticket.* Newspapers have *jackets* big enough to hold full page ads. On the other hand, a *dust jacket* is the paper cover of a hardcover book.

*Double-truck.* A two-page newspaper advertisement. Metal type pages are assembled on individual *trucks* that will take their considerable weight. Thus a two-page ad requires two of the trucks and is called a double-truck. Two-page paste-up ads are joined and are taped to large sheets of stiff plastic which are called *turtles,* but are still called double-trucks.

*Dummy.* Usually a pasteup of proofs in page position for makeup from galleys. To *dummy-up* is to mark the galley number on each paragraph of one set of the galley proofs. When it is cut apart and pasted into a dummy the compositor will know on which galley to find the type. A dummy may be anything from a rough sketch of the location of stories or ads to a precise drafting of positions. A *layout* is the same thing but precedes the typesetting.

*Edition.* A periodical publication of a certain date rarely has a lone version. The *New York Daily News,* for instance, changes regularly from 6 p.m. till 2 a.m. and later if necessary, and in addition prints different editions for northern and central New Jersey, Manhattan, Bronx, Brooklyn, Staten Island and two sections of Queens. Small newspapers usually confine themselves to first and home editions. National magazines and the *Wall Street Journal* have different regional editions. Books have numbered editions, the edition number being carried with the title in bibliographies.

*Flop.* Used to indicate that a negative is to be printed with the wrong side in contact with the paper. Thus a photo of an auto headed toward the left would be shown headed right.

*Floor.* Printers are usually classified into three categories—operators, floormen and proofreaders. Floor includes all of the hand work and a floorman is sometimes dignified as a *compositor.* A proofreader normally moves his corrected proofs back through the original channels—operator to floor to proofroom but, if only hand corrections are necessary, the proofs can go directly to the floor or pasteup. It is a good idea to indicate floor corrections because the normal method of correcting linotype is to pick up a bundle of correction lines and insert them rapidly, thereby missing hand work.

*Font.* Literally, all of the characters in one size and weight of a typeface. Characters not included in a regular font are *sorts.*

*Form.* Any bundle of type, from a few lines tied up with string to a press form for a full sheet of as many pages as it will take.

*Format.* All of the things that go into the design of a publication—shape, size and style. Computer formats are coded instructions for computers to execute formats.

*Galley.* A steel tray holding loose lines of type or type forms. See *Proof.*

*Grain.* Paper is composed of short and long fibers with the long ones running in one direction, and this direction is the grain. Paper tends to curl with the grain. In label work, a label glued to a bottle should have the grain running up and down the bottle. Otherwise a tension is built up, causing peeling. Label specifications may include a double-headed arrow under the dimension that is to be the grain direction as 2″ x 3″.

$$\longleftrightarrow$$

*Greek.* A meaningless collection of vowels repeated at random word lengths for use in a proposed layout as character count and for judgment of type appearance.

*Grid.* A grid is normally an area broken up into horizontal and vertical areas. The Monotype grid is a frame holding mats for casting metal type or negatives for photographing type. Some photosetters use square grids for their negative fonts and some use *disks* which may also be referred to as grids. Newspapers use sheets of card stock for paste makeup which are printed with grids in non-reproducing blue ink. These are called grids, and the grid pattern shows picas and preshrinkage inches horizontally and columns and gutters vertically.

*Head.* A headline. The various kinds are self-explanatory for the most part. A *run-in head* is one that is part of the regular line of type but usually in a different face or boldface. *Subheads* go between paragraphs, either flush left or centered. A *sidehead* may be a flush left subhead or one set in the margin of the regular text measure. *Running heads* are the repeats of book or chapter titles at the top of book pages. A *kicker* is a line of a commentative tone set smaller and above a regular newspaper head. The name of a newspaper is the *masthead. Head-to-head* means type forms made up so that the tops of the forms adjoin.

*Hold.* There is usually more type set for a publication than is used. Type that may be used later is proofed under a slug "overmatter" with job and galley number. Some copy comes marked hold for a given *release date. Kill* means wipe out the computer storage or dump the type.

*Imprint.* As a verb, imprint usually means to add printing to a job that has been printed, as numbers or names to checks. An imprint may be a branch publishing name of a publishing house. It is also the approval to publish issued by the Roman Catholic Church (the Latin name is *imprimatur*).

*Lead.* Lead is about the most prolific word in English. In printing, it is specifically two points of space but, as a verb, can mean any given amount of space. Lead metal is actually a combination of metals. Dead metal goes into a *hellbox* for remelting. A *lead* is the beginning of a news story. *New lead* means to substitute a more recent version.

*Lockup* (noun), *lock up* (verb). A type form is a spongy thing, held together by gravity and bracing or string until it is placed in a chase or the bed of a press and *locked* solid. Most typesetting is intended for offset and has served its purpose once reproduction proofs are pulled so the proof presses can be used for temporary lockup. A proof of the locked-up form should be approved by the proofroom. Usually a foreman assumes respon-

sibility for the squaring of the form and quality of the reproduction
proofs, color register and so forth. Sometimes a reader does it.

*Makeup.* Any arranging of type, from adding space to preparing complete forms. Newspapers sometimes classify makeup as a
work classification. *Pasteup* is the makeup of phototype. A complete pasteup on *hard board* is called a *mechanical* in art departments. *Stripping* is the makeup of negatives for burning an offset
plate. Makeup of press forms is called *imposition* and the Typographical Union prefers that word to *stripping* for the offset process
also.

*Proof.* Any reproduction of type made for proofreading or
editing. A *galley proof* is usually the type as it comes out of the
machine with no makeup, but some spacing may be added or even
book pages made up on galleys. Galley proofs are also called
*roughs.* Proofs of phototype are usually made on some form of
electrostatic copying machine and sometimes called *Xeroxes.*
Proofs on transparent bases are *transparencies* or *tissues.* A *chaser
proof* is one containing last-minute changes. An earlier proof than
the final one may be used for this purpose and generally only the
new correction is intended. *Reproduction proofs* or *repros* are
proofs suitable for the camera. Newspapers call them *slicks.* The
offset equivalent of a press proof is the *blueline* or *brownline*—a
proof of the stripped negatives that is more accurate in size than
other forms of proofing. *Ozalid* proofs give positive proofing from
other positive proofs printed on non-opaque but not necessarily
transparent paper.

*Printer.* Anyone working at the printing trade including proofreaders. To the buyer of printing, the typesetting shop handling a
job is the *printer.* To newspaper editorial departments, printers are
members of a union whose jurisdiction they must be careful never
to infringe. A more specific term is *typesetter.* Typesetting shops
have taken to calling their companies *typographers.* Specifically a

typographer is a designer of printing. For those customers who don't have their own typographers, typesetters have *service desks,* manned by *markup men.* A printer deals with a *customer, agency, publisher* or *store.* An agency has a *client.* A newspaper deals with *advertisers.*

*Quad.* Quads are pieces of spacing material of various widths used in setting hand type. The linotype has em and en quads. On old linotypes a short line was filled by adding quads and space bands. Automatic devices to do the job were called *quadders.* To make a line flush left, right or centered is expressed as *quad left* and so forth. Although there are no quads involved, phototypesetter keyboards contain keys to order those operations and copy or proof markup uses QL, QR and so forth.

*Reverse.* A reverse is a negative. It need not be on film. It can be directly on paper. In printing, the result is a black area leaving the type image as white paper. Naturally any color of ink or paper can be used. The black area must be defined. This is usually done for preliminary proofing of pasteups by preparing art with the solid black area and a regular black-on-white proof of the type positioned inside it. After okay of the type it is reversed on camera and pasted onto the black area. If the black area is not defined it must be indicated on the proof. Even if it is, the proof must carry the notation "Reverse." A *dropout* is a film reverse used mostly in color work where, for instance, the type is to be printed yellow and the background blue. This is necessary where transparent inks are to be used.

*Run.* To print. Usually used in connection with advance copy or ads as "run on May 20" or "run three times." *ROP* means "run of press" as opposed to limited editions.

*Signature.* A book or magazine is put together by sheets containing a number of pages folded so that the pages are in order

and trimmed. The result of the folding and trimming of each sheet
is a signature. The last step in proofreading is checking the press
sheet that will become a signature for final corrections and page
sequence. Summing up the name, address, slogan, trade-mark and
so forth of a company can be called a *signature* but *logo* is used
more frequently.

*Slug.* One line of linotype. From this comes the verb *slug,*
meaning to check the first word of each line of a revised proof
to see that no lines have been lost or transposed in inserting
corrections. The guideline at the top of a galley or of a news story
is called the *slug line.* The story may be said to be *slugged* "Man
shoots . . ." giving the first words of the headline. In spacing
material a *slug* is six points deep, and the expression is often used
on copy for that amount of extra paragraph space.

*Type.* The most limited meaning of *type* is foundry type but
machine slugs can be called type and the word can be used to
distinguish type from plates. Phototype is also called type. See the
chapter on marks. *Coldtype* is used to distinguish between it and
all other forms of reproducible photographic material and metal
typesetting. The word is used mostly to describe the process used
in producing the typesetting.

*Velox.* A photographic copy of anything to be used for offset
printing. It comes from Eastman's old printing paper and very
likely will be some other kind of print but the name has stuck.

*Widow.* The last line of a paragraph if less than a full line.
Some define one as less than half a line. Neither should be used
at the top of a page or column.

*Work the hook.* Copy to be set is still often hung on a hook
and printers are supposed to take jobs in order, not search for
something they prefer. This is just as rigorously enforced in the

proofroom wherever there is more than one reader and no one delegated to distribute work. An exception is urgent work. Failure to move a job that must be delivered can be a more serious fault than any proofreading error.

*Work and turn, twist or tumble.* These are press terms, but the makeup of forms for presses depends on how they are to be printed and readers may need to understand the reason for positioning the forms. *Work and turn* means printing the second side of a sheet by turning it over. A simple example is a single sheet printed on both sides. It could be done by printing one side and then changing the form and printing the other side. It is simpler to print both front and back forms at once and then turn the paper over and print the other side so that the back sides back up the front sides. The forms can be head to head, side by side or foot to foot. *Work and tumble* also involves turning the paper but a different form is used on the second side as in signatures of book pages. *Work and twist or twirl* involves overprinting, for instance making up a form having both horizontal and vertical rules as two forms. The forms are run at the same time. The paper is then twisted and run through the press again so that each form overprints the other. This is easier in the preparation of metal forms but for offset work it is easy to rule verticals by drawing or make acetate overlays. It could be useful in adding an extra color.

# 18

# Conditions
# of Employment

Now, SOME WORD on the working conditions and pay of proof-readers is in order.

These two factors are usually in inverse proportion. The typesetting shops, mostly unionized and working two or three shifts, are generally crowded, dirty, noisy, too hot or too cold, and bathed in lead fumes. The readers are paid the highest wages.

Conversely, a reader for a corporation, advertising agency or publisher, while perhaps getting something less than a living wage, may have his own personal desk or office in a well-kept, air-conditioned, modern building.

The non-union reader in a typesetting shop is worst-off. He has neither the pay of the union reader nor the working conditions of the office reader. His pay and security are dependent upon his ability on the job and courage in negotiating his own wages.

Conditions in the shops are improving as phototypesetting equipment is installed. Computers simply refuse to work if temperature and humidity are not ideal. Photographic materials are affected by temperature and dirt.

The animal environmental complex is an invisible and unsolvable problem. When a reader occupies a desk just vacated by another and in turn yields to another or, worse still, is shunted to another place to work by overtime crowding, he suffers an indignity no animal will permit without at least a snarl. Overhead and high investment in equipment make this necessary. Some employers aggravate the situation with a game of musical chairs— never enough facilities for the maximum work force.

Noise is the greatest annoyance with which a reader must cope and one which could be easily alleviated, but rarely is. The studies on damage to health, hearing and the nervous system by noise have been widely publicized but the simple remedy of enforcing rules against individual noisemakers is rarely used. A shop or newspaper where any attempt has been made to shield the readers from shop noises is a rarity, although all business offices of plants are so designed. There is a growing tendency to permit employees to bring radios to work and play them at volumes high enough to override the normal machine noises.

The greatest health hazard of the occupation is probably lead poisoning from the fumes of the molten lead in the typecasting machines. This was noted early in the century along with the same complaint by painters working with lead paints. It is now not measurable or provable because of workmen's compensation laws. A printer's death, pronounced due to this cause, would open the way to countless large suits against the insurers.

The most noticeable physical effect produced by the occupation is obesity, and alcoholism is not uncommon. The latter can stem partly from nervous tension induced by the work. The effect of the heavy eyestrain has not been measured but from observation does not appear to be serious. Reading from the cathode ray tube may be dangerous. Respiratory complaints are common but usually traceable to smoking.

As to physical qualifications, proofreading has few and is an ideal occupation for the crippled, the elderly or the heart-attack victim. There is actually too little physical effort involved for maintaining muscle tone and flexibility of the hands, arms and legs.

There are too many factors affecting wages to mention any

exact figures. Differentials occur regionally, by size of city, by union coverage and inflation. Even union scales in the South run less than half what they are in New York, Chicago and other metropolitan printing centers. They are becoming very uniform throughout California.

The best comparison of wage rates in the open market is with other kinds of jobs. Offerings for minimal experienced readers run slightly above general office clerical employees, including the lower echelon receptionists and secretaries, but lower than the personable or skilled in the latter two occupations. Likewise, in industrial work the reader only receives somewhat higher pay than the helper, attendant or assembly worker. Experienced and responsible readers can double this.

According to management theory, our school system produces more ready-made proofreaders than there is demand for. Only underpaid readers really believe this. The fact is that there is an aptitude requirement for reading, just as there is for music, mechanics or math. Experience with a large number of copyholders will show that very few can read without constantly substituting or omitting words. They may speak the common phrases with the tongues of angels but cannot note a twist in phraseology. Most will not differentiate between *has* and *had* or *a* and *an*. The more adept a person may be at rapid reading—getting the message out of a mass of unnecessary wordage—the more useless he will be at proofreading.

Anyone with the capability and inclination to accept the discipline of proofreading is a rare find. The one who is such a rarity can demand and receive a great deal more than is normally offered. What may seem like considerably more to the reader is as of no consequence to an employer in the printing and publishing industry. A single mistake can be more costly than his annual wage. In a few minutes of proofreading the reader approves typesetting exceeding in cost his wage for the day, and the ultimate use of the type can multiply this astronomically. A page ad in a few national magazines can exceed a million dollars in cost.

To get more pay a reader must be prepared to look for and

accept better offers—with confidence in his competence to do the work. There is psychological pressure against doing so—fear of the unknown, a too-modest appraisal of the value of his work, a lack of knowledge of employment opportunities.

Finding employment can be approached in several ways. Newspaper classified advertising is the most common source of jobs. The *New York Times* consistently offers a number of jobs. All jobs are not advertised by any means. Some companies prefer screening of applicants by agencies.

In cities where there is a considerable printing industry there will be an association of employers. In New York it is called the Employing Printers Association, in Chicago the Franklin Society. They usually have their own free agencies for all jobs in the industry.

Unions with closed shops have employment bureaus for their members only. The Newspaper Guild sometimes operates employment counseling but metropolitan papers have personnel departments. There are state and federal laws against refusal to hire for lack of union membership, which are avoided by asking about previous experience if the applicant does not immediately present his union card.

Situation-wanted ads are not very productive but may be indicated for those in places where employment opportunities are scarce. In addition to newspapers there are many trade journals that carry both situation-wanted and help-wanted ads.

City, state and federal agencies and the United Nations have many proofreading jobs. Usually they are under civil service and in the low clerical ratings, but if they are connected with printing plants they usually pay the going rates for the locality. The Typographical Union has jurisdiction in the U.S. Government Printing Office itself but not in other agencies.

In applying for civil service jobs the qualification requirements are basically related to previous experience which must be established by letters from previous employers stating satisfactory performance and length of employment. It is always advisable to obtain such a letter when leaving any job, even if not contemplating government work. Experience time is also a requirement for union membership.

With apologies for upsetting anyone's delicate religious sensitivity, it would be unfair not to mention that churches are heavily involved with employment opportunities and counseling, with contacts in unions and corporations and also owning printing shops, newspapers and publishing houses—openly or anonymously.

Getting deeper into the touchy area of prejudicial job practices, the battle of the sexes has been going on at a draw for a long time in the proofroom sector. With no physical requirement beyond eyesight involved, sex is hardly a hindrance to performance of the work. The ladies range from very attractive young ones to grandmothers (very attractive too, of course). In the most important area of proofreading—accuracy and spelling—they are equally competent with the men. Some states have regulations for women employees on the number of hours they are allowed to work and working periods. The Supreme Court has recently ruled against some such laws. However, women are apt to consider it unsafe to work at night in large cities and proofreading is an around-the-clock job. One problem characteristic is common to all woman readers. They will not tolerate a temperature below 80 degrees or the slightest draft.

There is a noticeable minority of blacks in the trade generally and especially in proofreading. However, competitive tests for apprenticeships are leading to a complete turnaround in racial percentages in spots. The New York School of Printing—a high school of printing jointly operated by the unions, employers and board of education—now has a high percentage of black students.

There is much more to be said on the subject and much better left unsaid. There will always be favoritism and prejudice concerning sex, race and religion in employment and the more attention focused on the matter, the more subtle the ways of practicing discrimination will become.

*The Unions.*

There are three unions that claim most of the jurisdiction over proofreading: The International Typographical Union (ITU), The Graphic Arts International Union (GAIU) and the Newspaper Guild.

These unions have had minor jurisdictional disputes in the past and have often refused cooperation with one another in contract disputes but have generally agreed on work classifications. The new equipment available for producing typesetting brought on a crisis that had not been resolved at the time of publication. Early in 1973 a great number of newspapers suddenly announced their intention to install optical recognition devices and place their operation in copy supplied by the advertising and editorial departments. The publishers have been persuaded by the young men selling the equipment that copy can be typed, corrections made in the typescript, and the scanners used to produce tape to operate the typesetting machines theoretically eliminating both typesetters and proofreaders. The commitment has been made. There will be enormous expense in unproven equipment, legal struggles, strikes and readjustments in working conditions.

The Newspaper Guild is an industrial union formed shortly before World War II to cover all otherwise unorganized newspaper employees. In most metropolitan centers the ITU claims and receives jurisdiction over the proofreaders. In some, and in the news magazines, the readers belong to the Guild. Newspaper copy editors, called "copyreaders," are in a definite editorial classification and there is only a minor difference in pay, if any at all, between them and the other editorial classifications, all of which generally exceed printers' scales.

The Graphic Arts International Union is a conglomerate that has emerged from mergers of the Lithographers, Bookbinders and other unions. It is moving toward absorption of the Newspaper Guild. The total membership at present is about 130,000 but the proofreader percentage is low. The union is industrial and negotiates, as the Guild does, by each job and by time on the job. A single plant may have several scales for readers.

So far the Teamsters Union hasn't made any publicized attempts at organization in the printing industry, but don't bet that they won't. There are runaway printing plants from the Jersey shore to the deep South and newspaper bastions that are successfully defying the traditional craft unions but would be vulnerable to the Teamsters' power over deliveries.

The ITU (International Typographical Union), which covers most proofreaders, is a craft union. That is, it claims jurisdiction over the printing craft in general. It has, with a few rare exceptions, maintained a single rate of pay for all members in a given shop, city or branch. The newspaper publishers and typesetters associations of a city usually negotiate as bodies for the newspaper scale and the book and job scale. Proofreaders are on an equal basis under the contracts with machine operators and compositors. The Women's Libbers should take note that equality has always existed in sex.

Beyond the union contract, members may negotiate for more than the union scale and, given differences in the quality of the work a shop produces, proofreaders often are bid for at rates even with or exceeding some of the other classifications.

A good non-union reader, working on proofs containing frequent typographical errors, and noting the ones in his newspaper, is apt to feel justifiable bitterness that he is working for as low as half of what the guilty union reader is getting in his protected state as a cardholder.

There are injustices in the system. There are many able readers working for much less than they are worth and union readers holding sinecures without effort or ability. For the most part, though, the union readers earn their pay. Newspaper errors are usually the result of hasty or no proofreading, and only a few printers have the proofreading and printing knowledge required by good typesetting plants. There are ways for non-union readers to become members.

The general position of the ITU on proofreading is that it has the right to jurisdiction and contract negotiators must do what they can to obtain it. The jurisdiction is specifically stated as, "All jobs must be proofread and revised by a journeyman." This doesn't prevent an editor or even a bookkeeper from also proofreading the job.

The law on membership in the union is that a member must be a qualified "practical printer" with at least six years experience at the trade. However, it takes a realistic attitude toward the necessity for specialization in certain jobs, including proofreading.

Preferably, membership is attained through the apprentice program—work at the trade combined with schooling, either in the printing schools maintained in the largest cities or mail courses from the International's Bureau of Education.

The law on six years experience is maintained but can be satisfied by any employment in the printing trade. There are many ways of meeting the ability qualifications. A primary factor is agreement of an employer to grant a proofreader journeyman status. One reason that employers are loath to agree to proofreading jurisdiction is that they are fearful of not being able to obtain well-qualified readers. There is, in some locals, a permit system by which non-members may hold union jobs on a limited-time, probationary basis. If the employer is satisfied with their work they may become members.

While the "practical printer" requirement—usually meaning that the member must be qualified as a compositor or operator—may be waived, a reader who is not so qualified is by no means assured of obtaining or holding a job. In union shops the priority laws grant any member the right to claim any job he is qualified to fill in the event of a reduction in force. Thus, operators and compositors may claim proofreaders' jobs, while the readers who are not qualified to do so may not claim the others' jobs.

In obtaining work, a reader is as much limited to his experience qualifications as a union member as he would be if he were not one. In some newspapers he will be granted the right to employment as a substitute upon presentation of his card. In many shops, however, he may be required to prove his ability on the floor, making up type. In the typesetting shops employment is mostly dependent upon previous reading experience, although some shops set up a combination classification of compositor-reader. Such a shop is apt to be more interested in high production than quality and will not offer much security against the inevitable loss of accounts.

Union readers are usually hired on a 30-days-trial basis. They may be discharged as incompetent during that period but thereafter only for cause. Many corporations operate in this way for all employees. In union shops discharge is usually effected by means of the layoff for lack of work. A reader who is laid off may accept work elsewhere or report for work daily. If he reports for work and is not hired by the day the employer is somewhat limited in his right to transfer other classifications into the proofroom.

The Typographical Union is over 120 years old. It began in 1850 when there were still laws making it a felony to conspire to form an association of workers. The printers held their first meetings in churches for sanctuary and for that reason the basic shop unit is called a "chapel." Several generations fought nobly to establish the union and get better wages and working conditions by small increments. There are still fights to the finish—strikes that bankrupt both newspapers and printers.

During most of its history there was little change in the work. Men started as apprentices and learned the typesetting skills which shielded them from unskilled competition. Today the trend is toward removing the necessity for individual craftsmanship from the bulk of typesetting through typewriter keyboards connected to computers. Although the sophisticated devices are more expensive than old methods they offer management a weapon to counteract the union's strongest one—know-how. At the finishing stage, makeup of pages and ads and setting of words and display lines, a great deal of jurisdiction has been lost to the art departments.

The structure of the ITU is not unlike that of the medical and bar associations. At the top is the executive council of the International, composed of the elected officers. It charters local unions in the United States and Canada. It rules on appeals from locals, has approval rights concerning contracts negotiated by the locals, and manages pension funds and the war chests for strike benefits.

International and local officers are elected by vote of the entire membership from a choice of nominees, usually two, for each office. All actions of the executive committee and changes in laws are subject to an annual convention of delegates from the locals. Some actions are restricted to a referendum vote by the entire membership of the union. Locals formulate their own laws and negotiate their own contracts within the laws of the International. They also have the checks of executive committees, action of the membership meetings and referendums.

Publication of detailed financial reports is required of both the International and the local unions.

Union or non-union, the educational requirements for proofreaders are generally at the high school graduate level. Some corporations are beginning to demand college degrees but are apt to realize that good experience is of greater importance. Experience also overrides age except in mandatory insurance requirements and federal law on age equality in hiring nullifies those. It is difficult and not very promising to break into the editing field without a college degree.

Security clearance is a frequent requirement for proofreaders, especially since a proofreader is one person who has a total "need to know" of the entire spectrum of classified publications. Clearance involves finger-printing and complete disclosure of one's past employment, home addresses, organization memberships, and military and criminal records. Clearance is most generally required in cities where there is heavy war materials production. Applications for clearance are now routed through the prime contractor to the branch of service involved. There is the quite natural supposition that the secrecy involved is between the branches of service and the companies seeking the defense contracts. The proofreader is bound to secrecy by national law, however.

Aside from governmental secrecy, a proofreader is ethically and sometimes contractually bound to hold anything he proofreads in confidence.

Since it is possible to earn as adequate a salary at proofreading as the Internal Revenue Service will allow, many devote their entire working lives to the job. There is a gamble involved in doing so, because of the possibility of acquiring eye injury or disease that may leave one without other qualifications for employment. There is also a continuing weakening of the principal union, the ITU.

Adjacent jobs to proofreading should be noted and training in them sought. In the publications a progression to editorial assistant is the normal move. In the shops it is toward typesetting skills. The operation of a teletypesetter keyboard is a killer job itself that progressively eliminates the operators but there are other special skills like camera and makeup that can be learned. Printing production offers considerable opportunities. Top jobs require complete college degrees but in certain metropolitan centers there are specialized courses that qualify people for satisfactory jobs.

It isn't easy. The tax collectors won't give any kind of break to the person attempting to learn about anything except his own specific job. If you are already getting some income from proofreading you can deduct the price of this book safely, but if you have to pay tuition or lay out money for any of the other expenses connected with improving your lot it's a no-no.

Your fellow workers will be loath to pass on any information about the tricks of their trades unless you have too much personality to waste it on honest employment.

Any reader who is more open-hearted toward imparting information or has dissenting opinions is welcome to write to the author, in care of the publisher. Who knows? There might be another edition.

# Index

AA's (author's alterations), 40, 97

Abbreviations: capitalization of, 51; and periods, 87; plural, 61; of proofreading marks, 23-25

Accents: and copyholder, 43, 45; marking of, 27

Addresses: commas used in, 84; typography for, 91; zip codes included in, 92-93

Advertising: and codes for reply mail, 93; costs of, 38, 39; legal restrictions on, 101-02; setting of dollar amounts in, 92; white space in, 113

Advertising agency, 38; taglines for, 94

Agate, 104

Airport Black typeface, 136

Akzidenz Grotesk typeface, 138

Alphatype, 31, 110, 125

Alts (author's alterations), 40, 97

Ampersand, and copyholder, 45

Apostrophe: adjustment of, in typography, 65; and copyholder, 44; use of, 61, 63, 64, 65

Ascenders, 135

Asterisk, and copyholder, 45

Author's alterations, 40, 97

"Ballot box," see Em

Baskerville typeface, 134, 140, 141

Bauer foundry, 144

Bodoni typefaces, 140, 143, 144

"Bogus," 39

Boldface: and copyholder, 44; wavy underscoring for, 26

Books: italics for titles of, 66; specifications for, 29, 94

Brackets, use of, 22